Freeform
Crochet
and beyond

BAGS · CUSHIONS · HATS · SCARVES · AND MORE

RENATE KIRKPATRICK

SALLYMILNER
PUBLISHING

First published in 2008 by
Sally Milner Publishing Pty Ltd
734 Woodville Road
Binda NSW 2583 AUSTRALIA

© Renate Kirkpatrick 2008
Reprinted 2010
Reprinted 2011

Design: Anna Warren, Warren Ventures Pty Ltd
Editing: Anne Savage
Photography: Tim Connolly
Illustrations: Wendy Gorton

Printed in China

National Library of Australia Cataloguing-in-Publication data:

Author:	Kirkpatrick, Renate, 1951-
Title:	Freeform crochet and beyond : bags, cushions, hats, scarves and more / Renate Kirkpatrick.
Publisher:	Binda, N.S.W. : Sally Milner Publishing, 2008.
ISBN:	9781863513852 (pbk.)
Series:	Milner craft series
Subjects:	Crocheting.
	Crocheting--Technique.
	Crocheting--Patterns
Dewey Number:	746.434041

Disclaimer

Information and instructions given in this book are presented in good faith, but no warranty is given nor results guaranteed, nor is freedom from any patent to be inferred. As we have no control over physical conditions surrounding application of information herein contained in this book, the author and publisher disclaim any liability for untoward results.

10 9 8 7 6 5 4

Acknowledgements

Thank you to my long-suffering family and friends who have patiently endured my many enthusiastic obsessions over the years with such good humour and grace.

A special thank you to my niece Tamran for her editing skills—nothing seems to escape her keen literary eye.

Sincere and heartfelt thanks must go to my students, both past and present, for their steadfast loyalty and encouragement—for asking the questions and making me search for the answers—I am truly grateful.

Thank you also to Libby Renney and her staff at Sally Milner Publishing for once again affording me this tremendous opportunity and providing me with their expertise, advice and ongoing support.

Aspirations for this publication

My aim with this book is to encourage the reader to tap into the hidden creativity that, I believe, lurks within us all—to entice the true beginner with easy starting points that will then lead them on to explore other techniques and experiment with what they learn, free from too many rules and must-nots—and, for the more experienced, to call upon all the arts and crafts that he or she has explored over the years, in some cases abandoned, and bring them together in a truly amazing art form.

Dedication

to all those creative individuals who think outside the square, who have the courage to display their eccentricities with flair and who dare to be different

Contents

1.
Basic freeform techniques

Incorporate every stitch you've ever learnt, together with the exciting colours and variety of yarns available today, mix in a little imagination and you've found the key to this fascinating technique of freeform.

No matter what level of skill you're at, or how creative you believe yourself to be: if you allow colour, texture and form to lead the way … intuition, spontaneity and the sheer joy of doing to be your guide, freeform can take you on a fascinating adventure.

At the risk of sounding clichéd, from the very beginning the Australian environment has been my inspirational guide: the colours, forms and textures of our flora and fauna, landscapes and oceans never cease to amaze and excite the artist in me.

A few years ago one of my students burst into class overflowing with excitement about a new crocheting/knitting technique where no rules apply and anything goes. No rules? Anything goes? How can that be? Intrigued, I jumped on the Net the moment I got home and discovered the fascinating world of scrumbling (also known as freeform). Where had I been hiding all this time not to know about this exciting direction crochet and knitting were taking? Totally captivated, I couldn't wait to give it a go. I floundered around on my own for a while, then attended an awe-inspiring workshop with Prudence Mapstone and I've been hooked (pardon the pun) ever since. So began my journey into colour, texture and artistry. As time passed and my experience grew I was encouraged to include freeform workshops in my teaching repertoire.

For me, freeform has become an all-consuming creative art form—a fascinating vehicle for self-expression—while yarns have become my palette; needle and hook my pencil, crayon and brush. It's a truly liberating technique relying entirely on the imagination. More often

than not I'm guided by the colour or texture of a yarn rather than the project itself. For example, I may have a bag in mind—but as my patches come together a beret may look better, and so I go along that path. I'm never absolutely sure how it will turn out but I'm always surprised and excited by the result.

This open-minded approach, allowing your project to grow and evolve, applies to almost every project featured in this book. Even though I may use a template with the aim of defining the basic shape for, say, a vest, there is nothing stopping me from adding sleeves, a collar or extra length if I feel the garment will look and/or fit better.

This of course applies in reverse also—for example, I'm well on my way to completing a coat, I've been placing my patches this way and that over the template and no matter how many times I leave and come back for another look, it's simply not working. Instinct tells me it's never going to work—perhaps it's going to be too weighty and overbearing, perhaps my colour choice is becoming far too over-the-top, even by my standards. Okay, that's fine, there's no need for panic. I shorten the length, take away the sleeves and open up the neckline and suddenly it all falls into place—I have a great looking vest. The extra patches won't be wasted because I'll use them in other projects or they may even prompt the beginning of a whole new idea. I believe that if you allow yourself this freedom of design it will stimulate the latent creativity that's hiding beneath the surface—bursting to get out. It will surprise and delight even the most staid of us.

Stitch patterns and templates

Although I include written and drawn **stitch patterns** to help students get started, to guide and stimulate ideas, there are no hard and fast rules as to how any stitch pattern should be used. In my experience no two people will produce the same result even when they follow the same stitch pattern to the letter. An artist by nature but a teacher at heart, my main aim is to encourage students to be spontaneous, trust their intuition and never stop asking themselves, 'I wonder what will happen

if I try this or that?' and then give it a go. The results aren't always as expected, but more often give a fresh perspective to the work, sometimes producing something so special it becomes the centrepiece of the project.

Templates are used as guides for the basic shape of a project. For example, a template for a bag can be as easy as folding a rectangular sheet of paper in half. Take another look at your old dressmaking patterns or buy new modern ones—you'll be delighted with this treasure trove. Stitch your patches to an existing garment like a T-shirt. Pull apart an old favourite jumper and use it as a template. My main advice here is to keep templates simple, preferably staying away from gussets, darts and inlays, at least in the beginning.

Skill requirements

Although freeform can be worked exclusively in either crochet or knitting, combining the two produces the most interesting results. Even with limited skills you'll be able to create the most amazing effects. Moreover, I'm not a purist and I urge students to use whatever skills they've acquired over the years—embroidery, felting, weaving, quilting, to name a few—which can, in one way or another, be incorporated into their freeform project to create something that is genuinely unique.

Choosing colour and texture

Think about what you want to make (bag, cushion cover, garment) and the colour range you'd like to work in. Collect as many yarns as you can (at least 15 to 20, but the more the better) and any colours and/or textures you think may work well together: thick, thin, smooth, textured, mohair, metallic, cotton, wool, synthetic. The wider your colour and texture ranges the more interesting effects you'll achieve. Obviously, good quality yarns produce good quality results. However, I use all kinds of fibre blends and never shy away from using economy yarns if they will produce the colour and/or texture and/or effect I'm after. Since most projects will only ever be hand-laundered, and very

infrequently ironed, fibres in combination are rarely in conflict. If you feel there's going to be a problem, there's no reason why you can't make up small swatches beforehand and give them a vigorous workout to determine how the colour/dye/texture holds up.

Go through your scrap basket. That must-have, couldn't-live-without yarn you loved so much in the store but which was at odds with what you already had and never found a use for may suddenly become the jewel in the crown.

Most people have a favourite colour scheme and for the beginner I would suggest staying within the realm of what you know and where you're comfortable. However, as you gain more experience this will soon become too limiting. You'll get the urge to experiment—you won't be able to help yourself.

Experimenting with colour/texture/form/stitches is the key. Stepping out of the square becomes a natural progression—the beginning of the great adventure.

Tools

The tools couldn't be simpler—all you need is a variety of crochet hooks (ordinary and Tunisian) and knitting needles in all sizes (whatever you have); a darning needle (plus an extra one in case the first one is lost); a tape measure; safety pins and ordinary pins; scissors—and that's about it.

For those of you who want to explore and incorporate other techniques (embroidery, felting, etc.) into your work, the tool requirements are listed in Chapter 7.

Tension

I am often asked how to gauge the tension throughout the work—to be honest, it's not something I worry about. If the yarn is too heavy or light for the hook or needle I'm using, I simply go up or down a size. Sometimes I'll work with a large hook and fine yarn, even odd-sized needles. It all depends on the effect I'm trying to create.

Do I crochet or knit?

Again, it's up to you. I am far more experienced in crochet so I tend to crochet more than knit. But I've found that a bit of knitting (mainly garter stitch) interlaced with crochet will help a garment drape better; on the other hand, hats and bags, which require a tighter finish, can be worked in crochet alone. There really are no hard and fast rules, which is why experimenting with stitches and yarns is so beneficial—you'll never know until you have a go.

Markers

Short loops of yarn for markers are helpful to easily identify the top/bottom or right/wrong side of your patch.

Blocking

Do not block freeform work using conventional methods. Heat and steam will demolish its sculptural aspect. As well, the combinations of yarns used may react adversely to each other—acrylics lose body, wool can felt, nylon and metallic can melt. It's not worth the risk.

For those who feel blocking their work is necessary, I recommend the following: using rust-proof pins, secure your project into shape onto a terry towel on a flat surface, then apply spray starch liberally and allow to dry completely.

Storing your yarns

As you begin your journey you'll be content to use the yarns you've collected over the years. Then a particular project will prompt a new purchase, and others will be picked up here and there as you come across them. Before long you'll have quite a collection and find yourself rummaging through the lot trying to find that hot pink you know is in there somewhere. At least that's how it was for me before I discovered the plastic-lidded fat-quarter bags favoured by quilters. My colours are now neatly stored together and the clear plastic lids let me instantly view the contents. Of course, you may not want to spend money on containers when the same money could be spent on yet more yarn. So have a look around the house and consider boxes, bins, bags, even plastic interlocking trays that might do the job.

Staying the master; keeping control

I prefer keeping my patches small, about palm size, and usually work on a few at the same time. For example, if I'm using red, I might pick up a few stitches on one patch and knit a bit, work a bullion on a previous one, and a surface chain to hide a join on yet another. In this way I'm moving the red around. I keep my template close, placing the patches here and there for colour and texture distribution and to ensure they remain flat.

If you allow it, freeform can take off in directions you couldn't even begin to anticipate. You get so engrossed that you suddenly find that endearing, vivid lime green has taken over! You have a couple of drastic options—pull the lot out and never go there again, or continue and donate the calamity to the next school fete.

But, before despair gets the better of you, let me make a suggestion— put your work aside for the minute, make yourself a cuppa—take a deep breath—take the dog for a walk. Then when you come back, have another look; I'm sure you'll find it's not really as bad as you first thought.

And, since you've already invested so much time into your project, doing one or other of these things might be a far better idea:

- Work more of the lime green on other patches to convince the eye it's meant to be there after all.

- Bombard it with buttons and beads.

- Surface embellish using hairy or loopy yarn.

- Make a separate motif and stitch it on so it partially covers the area.

- If the piece you're working on is too big or flyaway, you could overlap, fold or pleat it—even gather it together like a drawstring.

Above all, don't panic! Your project is not ruined, it just needs some creative adjustments. There's always a way round these little trials and who knows—what you think of as disaster today may well turn out to be a triumph tomorrow.

Bringing in a new yarn or colour

Most of you will be familiar with joining yarn with a slip stitch (ss), which is technically correct. However, I find it more economical, both in time and yarn, to simply bring it in. For example, for a surface embellishment—with right side facing, I draw up a loop on the base fabric from where I want to work, then proceed with the pattern and, wherever possible, work over the tail end as I go.

Changing colour or yarn when working stitches

Regardless of what stitch you are working, always bring in new yarn or colour when 2 loops of the last working colour remain on hook, drop working colour, pick up new colour and draw through 2 loops. This method applies at the beginning and end of rows/rounds and anywhere in between.

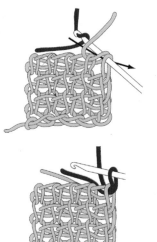

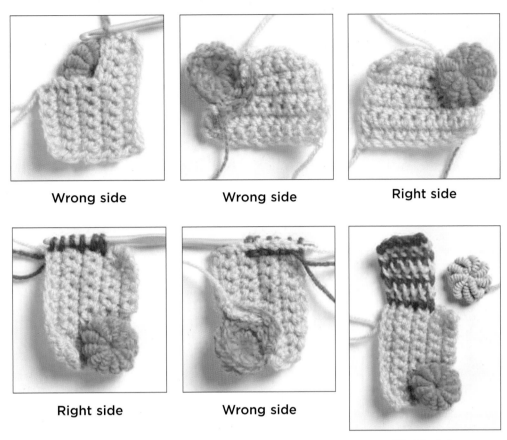

Wrong side   Wrong side   Right side

Right side   Wrong side   Right side

Picking up stitches and joining round motifs

Wherever possible, work directly into the patch either by slip seaming an existing motif into a space or picking up a few stitches and knitting/crocheting for a while. This saves a lot of sewing in later and patches grow more quickly.

Slip seam: do not finish off motif just made, remove hook, with wrong side of patch to be joined facing, insert hook where required, pick up dropped loop and draw through, insert hook a couple of stiches forward through patch and through next stitch on motif, yoh and draw up a loop through motif, patch and loop on hook—slip seam made.

Tying up loose ends

Frequent changes of colour or yarn will create a multitude of loose ends or tail ends. Wherever possible it's a good idea to knit or crochet over them as you work. Others should be regularly woven in with a darning needle. Keeping a check on loose ends saves on a huge job at the end—assuming, of course, that you want the ends gone. You may be inclined to make a feature of them—in which case, bring them to the right side and cut them to size accordingly. You could even add a bead or two.

Joining patches

As a general rule, don't join patches too soon or at least until about three-quarters of the template area is covered. This leaves you free to move patches around until the distribution of colour/texture/form is right (for you).

When you have enough patches and you've moved them around this way and that, the colours and textures are evenly placed and balanced, and you're happy with the overall effect, you're ready to start joining. Don't worry if there are holes, they will be filled in later.

MATTRESS STITCH (LADDER ST)

- Thread a blunt-ended darning needle with a yarn that tones in and, with right side facing, join in at the back on one edge.

- Slide the needle through 2 loops of one patch then 2 loops of the other.

- Repeat a couple of times and draw together firmly.

- Gently, manually ease the stitches back with your fingers.

- Continue until the join is complete.

- Lay your work down often to ensure that it is staying flat.

For demonstration purposes I've used a contrasting yarn—even so, you can see the mattress stitch join is almost invisible.

As you work you'll find your patches don't always fit snugly together and even more gaps and holes seem to appear—don't worry, all will be well. It's better to leave a hole than to pull the work too tight. At this stage you're only interested in getting the basic shape right.

And don't dismiss crocheting your joins together either. I do this often, using a loopy or hairy yarn, or crab stitching with metallic thread, to make a feature of the join itself.

Filling in the holes

So, your patches are joined and you are now the proud owner of a whole new piece of fabric and, even though it's full of gaps and holes, you can see that your project is really beginning to take shape. Now, knit or crochet shapes or motifs appropriate for the spaces (it's worth remembering that round motifs go easily into square holes) and slip seam or mattress stitch them into place. Use popcorns and domes to fill those tiny, difficult holes. When they're all filled, you're ready to bead or embroider or add those extra bits and pieces that will make your project your own.

Lining

I usually don't bother lining garments or hats. Besides being extra work, I find it interrupts the drape of the garment. Tail ends that are woven in neatly and securely are barely noticeable on the wrong side. But of course this is purely personal, and if you prefer lining your project it's entirely up to you.

Bags, of course, are different and need individual assessment. As a general rule, I find it's helpful to have a 'base' at the top of the bag frame. It gives me somewhere to attach both the lining and my patches. So, depending on the effect I'm after, I may work a long dc (US sc) stitch using a fuzzy yarn or even two yarns together around the opening of the bag. Alternatively, I might bring the lining up and over the rim of the opening and attach my patches to this. The style of bag, type of handle, fastener or frame used will all determine how I should finish off.

Ways of finishing a bag opening.

Beading

When I'm beading defined areas (beading tassels is different; see Chapter 6), I prefer to do it last thing—only after all the patches have been joined, holes filled in and I'm ready to attach the fabric to the frame. This enables me to place baubles and beads exactly where I want them—but again, if you prefer beading as you go then that's what you should do.

- For the best results use beading thread—it's strong, slightly elastic and less visible.

- Tie off your thread often—should a section of beads break, only that section will unravel.

- Use beads to highlight a dull colour or section.

Making a bag

SUGGESTED EXTRAS

Depending on your project you may need shade-cloth or rug canvas as a base or backing to attach your freeform fabric to, bag frames, handles, magnetic catches, lining, beads, beading needles and thread, buttons, filling for cushions, ribbon, cord, tassels.

Bags need a strong base. What a tragedy it would be if, after spending hours creating your lovely new handbag, it stretched, warped and sagged out of shape the moment you put in your purse, cosmetics and mobile phone. So give a thought to this fundamental requirement.

There are many styles of bag frame on the market (available in most good craft stores) to which your freeform patches can be attached. Those clever sewers out there could make their bag base using a durable fabric and attaching their freeform patches directly to the outside, which may even eliminate lining if desired. Another suggestion is to use an old existing bag and attach your freeform patches to that.

However, my preference is to use a lightweight shade-cloth (available in any hardware store and usually comes in beige, green and black). It's readily available, inexpensive and durable, pliable, washable and easy to machine and/or hand sew.

Preparing a shade-cloth bag base

- Cut out basic shape.

- Stitch seams and turn inside out if desired.

- Turn over seam allowance at top edge.

- With a complementary coloured and, preferably, textured yarn work long double crochet—Ldc (US Lsc)—around the top edge. This gives you an easy edge onto which to attach your completed patches and later the handles and lining.

LONG DOUBLE CROCHET—LDC (US LSC)

Insert hook into st or sp indicated, draw up a long loop even with st in working row, yoh and draw through 2 loops on hook—Ldc (US Lsc) made.

Assembling your bag

- Wrap and pin your freeform fabric around the shade-cloth base to see how it fits.

- Fill in holes and gaps at seams.

- Bead where desired.

- When all is how it should be; thread a blunt ended darning needle with a yarn that tones in and join on the inside starting at the base then with a long running stitch work your way evenly around and upward attaching the fabric to the shade-cloth.

- Attach the top edges in the same manner as joining patches (mattress st).

- Stitch in lining.

Note Adjustments must sometimes be made to the lining when attaching magnetic clips and handles.

FREEFORM BAG HANDLES

Work as tightly as possible, go down a hook size if necessary.

Using 2 yarns together, make 4 ch.

Row 1: (right side) dc (US sc) in 2nd ch from hook and in each ch across—3 dc (US sc)

Row 2 and subsequent rows: 1 ch, turn, dc (US sc) in each dc (US sc) across—3 dc (US sc).

Repeat Row 2 to desired length, do not finish off.

With right side facing, work crab st completely around, join to first crab st, finish off.

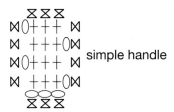
simple handle

Freeform bag handles, one made with a single thick yarn, the other with two thinner yarns together.

Summary of useful tips and tricks

- Decide on your colour scheme and collect your yarns accordingly. Keep in mind contrasts, harmonies and textures—the wider your range the more interesting effects you'll achieve. Don't be afraid to take risks—be adventurous!

- Keep the template for your project simple. Use self-designed or commercial dressmaker patterns as flat templates.

- Place patches down and around your template frequently as you work—always aim for harmony and the most effective colour and texture distribution. Your eye should wonder freely over your work. If it's constantly coming to an abrupt stop at a particular place or patch, take another look—adjustments to colour/texture/placement may be required.

- Place patches up to (but not over) the seam allowance. Work that is too short can be added to later.

- Keep track of the right side of your work; mark with a thread if necessary.

- Keep your patches small and change yarn colour and texture often.

- Keep checking that your work remains flat.

- Keep your work uniform by incorporating at least some of your yarns in each patch.

- Change hook and needle size appropriate to the yarn and/or the effect you're trying to achieve.

- Crochet/knit over tail ends wherever possible, and periodically weave in ends with darning needle to avoid that huge job at the end.

- Do not join your patches too soon so that you're free to move them around, add extra motifs or place those not-so-good bits in less obvious places like on a seam under the arm.

- Most importantly, enjoy yourself—allow the colours and textures to lead the way. Be intuitive and experiment—you'll be amazed how creative you actually are.

2.
Starters and more

Newcomers to the freeform technique find the concept of no rules, anything goes and all that's required is a bit of imagination, confusing, if not daunting. So, where to start?

I find the easiest way to begin, and quickly gain understanding of the technique, is to knit/crochet small starter patches: squares, triangles, rectangles or odd shapes that have been increased or decreased at will. These are then built on by picking up a few stitches along an edge in a new yarn and working in a different direction for a few rows, all the while being conscious of creating spaces/gaps/right angles where stitches/motifs can be attached later.

Of course, this is only a suggestion; nothing is set in stone. You can just as successfully begin with a round motif like a circle, double circle or bullion and build your patch from these. Why not try both and see which you prefer?

I recommend working in a random, haphazard fashion, changing direction/yarn/stitch often to avoid making neat geometric shapes. You'll find that odd shapes fit easily together like a jigsaw and the joins are less visible than straight lines.

The following examples are simple patch patterns to get you started. However, don't be restricted by them. Work in stripes, use different plies, odd-sized needles, two yarns at the same time, look at the wrong side. Sometimes, and this is particularly true for loopy or furry yarn, the back looks better than the front (this is where markers come in handy).

So you are now on your way but first, a quick reminder about the basic stitches you will be using. I hope you enjoy the adventure as much as I do.

STITCH GUIDE

Basic crochet stitches

Abbreviations

ch	chain
ss	slip stitch
dc (US sc)	double crochet (US single crochet)
tr (US dc)	treble (US double crochet)
htr (US hdc)	half treble (US half double crochet)
dtr (US tr)	double treble (US treble)
yoh	yarn over hook

SLIP KNOT

Use slip knots rather than just tying an ordinary knot—it's neater and allows the next chain (ch 1) to flow rather than being tugged through the loop just made. Never count the loop (on hook) as a chain or stitch.

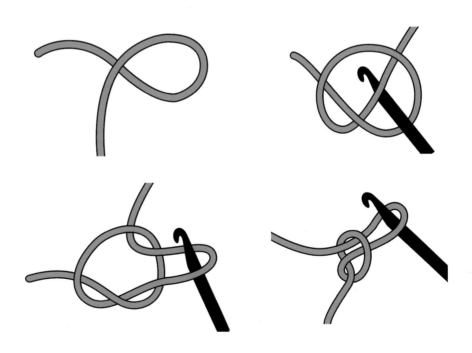

FOUNDATION CHAIN: CHAIN/CH

This means the number of chains required for length and/or pattern *plus* the extra chains that are required to accommodate the stitch height.

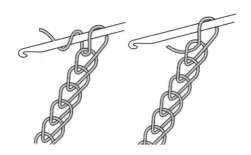

SLIP STITCH/SS

Insert hook into st, yoh and draw yarn through st and loop on hook.

DOUBLE CROCHET/DC (US SINGLE CROCHET/SC)

Working along foundation ch, insert hook into 2nd ch from hook, yoh and draw loop through st (2 loops on hook), yoh and draw yarn through both loops—dc (US sc) made.

HALF TREBLE/HTR (US HALF DOUBLE CROCHET/HDC)

Working along foundation ch, yoh, insert hook into 3rd ch from hook, yoh and draw loop through st (3 loops on hook), yoh and draw yarn through all three loops—htr (US hdc) made.

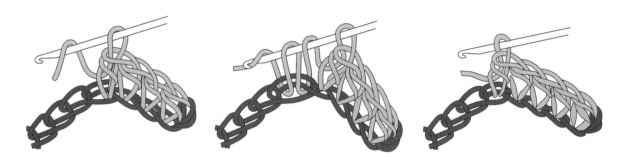

TREBLE/TR (US DOUBLE CROCHET/DC)

Working along foundation ch, yoh, insert hook into 4th ch from hook, yoh and draw yarn through st (3 loops on hook), yoh, draw through 2 loops, yoh and draw through last 2 loops—tr (US dc) made.

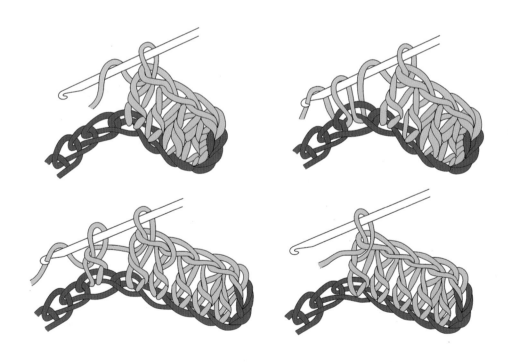

DOUBLE TREBLE/DTR (US TREBLE CROCHET/US TR)

Yoh twice, insert hook in st or sp and pull up a loop, yoh and draw
through 2 loops on hook 3 times.

FRONT OR BACK LOOP ONLY

Work only in loop indicated by arrow.

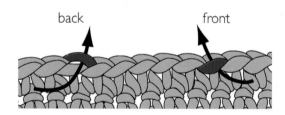

POST STITCH (FP OR BP)

Work around post of stitch indicated in row or rows below, inserting
hook in direction of arrow.

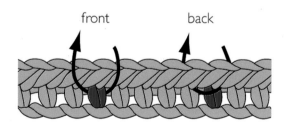

FINISHING OFF (CASTING OFF STITCH)

With the last stitch complete, cut yarn, and draw though the loop on hook, pull tight to close the loop. Weave in end. With slippery yarn, draw through the loop twice (make an extra chain) and pull down very tightly with your thumb to close. Weave in end.

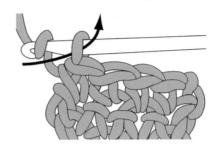

BEGINNING CLUSTER

3 ch, (yoh, insert hook in ring and pull up a loop, yoh and draw through 2 loops on hook) twice, yoh and draw through all 3 loops on hook.

CLUSTER

Yoh, insert hook in stitch or space and pull up a loop, yoh and draw through 2 loops on hook) 3 times, yoh and draw through all 4 loops on hook.

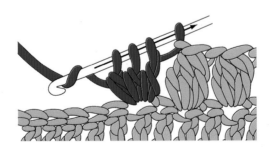

POPCORN

Work 5 tr or 5 htr (US 5 dc or 5 tr) in st or sp, drop loop from hook, insert hook in first st of group, hook dropped loop and draw through, 1ch to close.

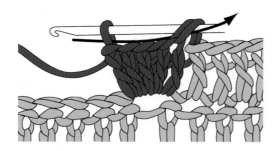

PUFF STITCH

(yoh, insert hook in st or space, yoh and pull up a loop even with hook) 3 or 4 times, yoh and draw through all 7 or 9 loops on hook, 1 ch to close.

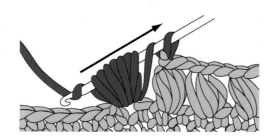

FREEFORM DIAGRAM SYMBOLS

⬭	chain (ch)
●	slip stitch (sl st)
†	double crochet (dc)
T	half treble (htr)
⊤	treble (tr)
⊤	double treble (dtr)
a b c	work in front loop
a b c	work in back loop
a b c d e f	front post
a b c d e f	back post
a b c	decrease
⊠	reverse dc (crab st)
⊠	reverse dc (crab st) in front loop
×	tunisian dc

|	tunisian loop/ knit st
O---------	tunisian return row
◀	finish off
◁	bring in new yarn or colour
⌒	unused loop
⟨ ⟩	row
a b	puff
⊕	beg cluster
a b c	cluster
coil st	coil st
a b	wrap or offset st
bullion with number of wraps	bullion with number of wraps
bent bullion with number of wraps	bent bullion with number of wraps
winding or limpet st	winding or limpet st

29

Basic Tunisian crochet

2nd bar   1st bar

FOUNDATION CHAIN/CH: NUMBER OF CHAINS
AS REQUIRED FOR LENGTH

One complete row is equal to:

- 1 pick-up row—you should have the same number of loops on hook
  as foundation ch.

- 1 cast-off row—you should be left with one loop on hook.

Row 1a: (pick-up row) insert hook in next ch, draw up a loop and leave
on hook, repeat across to end—same number of loops on hook as
foundation ch.

Row 1b: (cast-off row) yoh, draw through first loop on hook, *yoh,
draw through 2 loops on hook, repeat from * across until one loop
remains (this last loop is the first loop of the next pick-up row)

Row 2a: *insert hook under next vertical bar, yoh and draw up a loop,
repeat from * across to last vertical bar—same number of loops on hook
as foundation ch.

Row 2b: cast off as in Row 1b.

Repeat Rows 2a and 2b to desired size.

Last Row: use an ordinary crochet hook 1 or 2 sizes smaller than the
Tunisian/tricot hook and continue working in the vertical bars in either
dc or ss—1ch, dc/ss in very first bar and then in each bar across—
finish off.

Basic knit stitches

Abbreviations

st	stitch
k	knit
p	purl
ss	slip stitch
yon	yarn over needle

KNIT SLIP KNOT

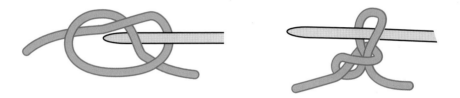

KNIT CAST ON

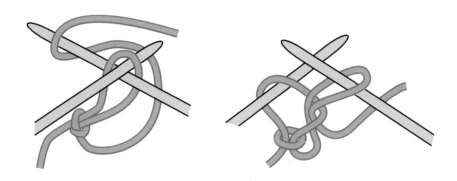

With slip knot on left needle, insert right needle, take yon and draw loop through to form a st, transfer this st to left needle, insert right needle into st just made, yon and draw through to form another st, transfer this new st to left needle, continue for the number of sts required.

KNIT STITCH

Hold yarn at back of work, insert right needle into front of first st from left to right, take yarn around right needle and draw loop forward to form a st, slide first st off left needle, continue with each st to end.

PURL STITCH

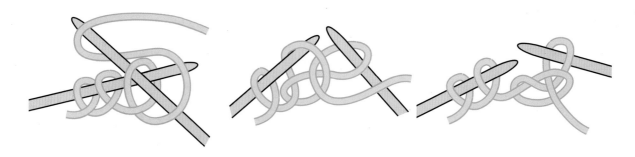

Hold yarn at front of work, insert right needle into front of first st from right to left, take yarn backward over right needle then forward and under, draw this loop backward to form a s, slide first st off left needle, continue with each st to end.

KNIT CASTING OFF

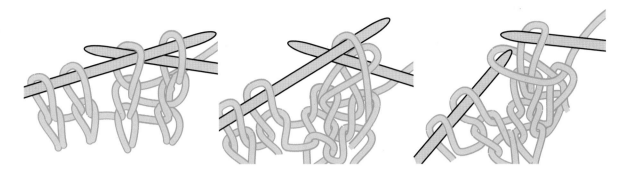

Work first 2 stitches, *pull first st over second stitch and off needle, work next st then repeat from * to end.

KNIT FINISHING OFF

After casting off, slip yarn through last stitch and pull tight to secure, weave in end with blunt darning needle.

STARTER PATCHES

Any of the following patches are suitable as basic starter elements.

Squares, rectangles and triangles

GARTER STITCH

Cast on 10 to 16 sts and knit a small square.

DOUBLE CROCHET (US SC) SQUARE

Make an uneven number of ch (11 to 17 ch), dc (US sc) in 2nd ch from hook and in each ch across (you should now have an even number of sts), *1 ch, turn, dc (US sc) in each dc (US sc) across, repeat from * until you have a small square.

   dc square

RECTANGLE

Using either of the above squares and with right side facing, in a different yarn pick up an uneven number of sts to about halfway along one edge and in the stitch of your choice knit/crochet a small rectangle in a plain colour, textured and/or in stripes. The idea is to create a space where an independent, round or odd-shaped motif could be placed later (see photo).

TRIANGLE

Using any of the above pieces, with right side facing and in a different yarn pick up an uneven number of sts to about halfway along one edge. Then in the stitch of your choice knit/crochet a small triangle by decreasing one st at beginning and end of each row in a plain colour, textured and/or stripes. The idea here again, is to create a space where an independent, round or odd-shaped motif could be placed later (see photo).

Alternatively, decrease your triangle on one side only.

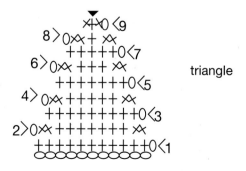

triangle

SUGGESTED STITCHES FOR SQUARES, RECTANGLES AND TRIANGLES

- knit: moss st, rib, stocking

- crochet: mesh, Tunisian, dc (US sc)

Shells and scallops

SHELLS

Shells are made by working a number of sts—3 to 7 dc (US sc), htr (US hdc) or tr (US dc)—in the one st or sp.

Work a number of shells along an edge in different colours and yarns or work a single shell to fill in a corner.

shells

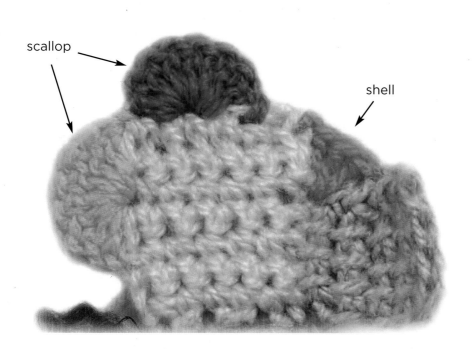

SCALLOPS

Work a single shell in the centre of a long edge. Then, changing yarn and joining in the appropriate st or sp, work a row of tr (US dc) or dc (US sc) along the same edge and over the first shell made. Repeat this row to desired effect, remembering to increase appropriately to keep work flat. Alternatively, work in back loops only and surface-embellish the unused loops later.

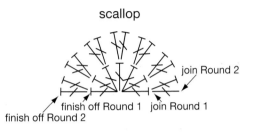

scallop

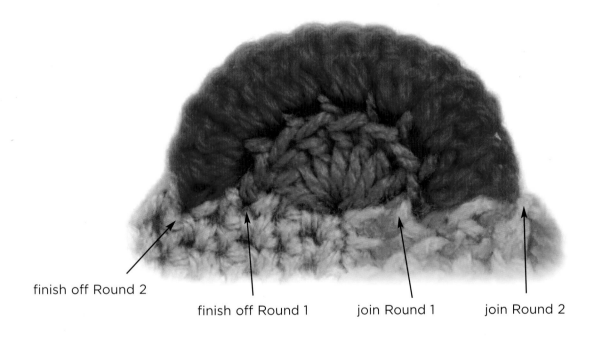

finish off Round 2

finish off Round 1

join Round 1

join Round 2

Round 1: 7 tr (US dc)

Round 2: 2 tr (US dc) in back loop of each st around

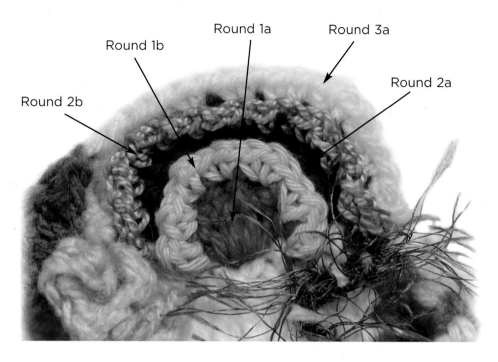

Round 1a: tr (US dc)

Round 1b: 2 dc (US sc) in each unused loop around

Round 2a: dc (US sc) in back loops of previous round

Round 2b: (dc [US sc], 1 ch, dc [US sc]) in each unused loop around

Round 3a: dc (US sc) in back loops of previous round

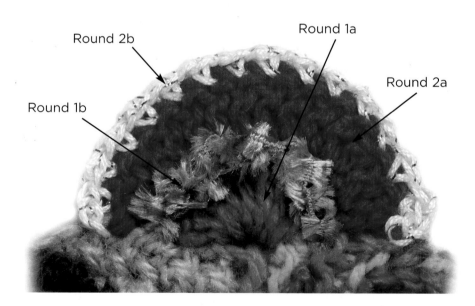

Round 1a: tr (US dc)

Round 1b: (ss, 1 ch) in each unused loop around

Round 2a: tr (US dc) in back loops of previous round

Round 2b: (de [US sc], 1 ch) in each stitch around

Spirals and circles

While shells and scallops can be worked directly on other shapes, round crochet motifs must be worked separately.

SPIRAL BASE

Using a plain yarn, make 3 ch and join with ss to form a ring, 1 ch, into ring work 8 dc (US sc) (for easy identification mark first st of round), do not join and using back loops only, work 2 htr (US hdc) into each dc (US sc) around to marker, do not join, then, again using back loops only, *work 2 tr (US dc) into next htr (US hdc), 1 tr (US dc) in next htr (US hdc), repeat from * around to marker, finish off. Alternately, taper off the spiral by reducing stitch size—that is, work a number of htr (US hdc) then dc (US sc) and finish off with ss.

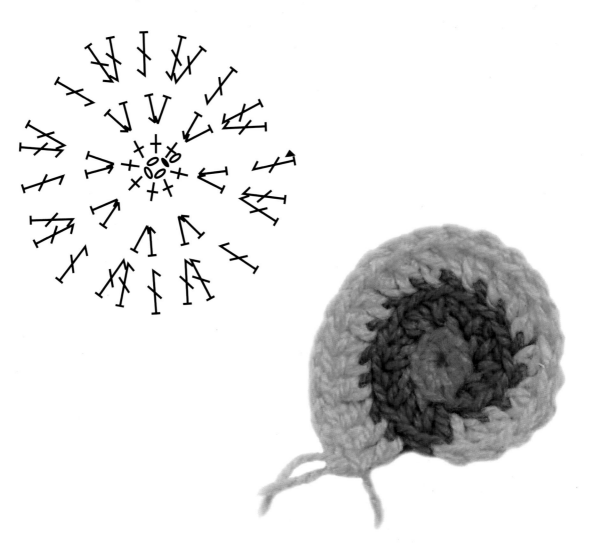

SPIRAL SURFACES

On their own, spiral bases are relatively uninteresting and usually require some surface embellishment. I like to use a finer yarn and appropriate hook and work each unused loop to produce a relief pattern. The following are but a few examples you can try.

Spiral surface 1

With right side facing and beginning from the centre, ss in each unused loop around.

Spiral surface 2

With right side facing and beginning from the centre, 1 ch, (dc [US sc], 1 ch) into each loop around to end, finish off.

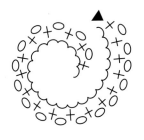

dc, 1ch
in unused loops
of spiral surface

Spiral surface 3

With right side facing and beginning from the centre, 1 ch, dc (US sc) in same loop, *(dc [US sc] in next loop, 3 ch, dc [US sc] in next loop), repeat from * around to end, finish off.

dc, 3ch, dc
in unused loops
of spiral surface

Spiral surface 4

With right side facing and beginning from the centre, 1 ch, dc (US sc), *work a 7 loop puff and 1 ch to close into next loop, dc (US sc) in next loop, repeat from * around to end, finish off.

dc & puffs
in unused loops
of spiral surface

PUFF STITCH

(yoh, insert hook in st or sp, yoh and pull up a loop even with hook) 3 or 4 times, yoh and draw through all 7 or 9 loops on hook, 1 ch to close.

MULTICOLOURED SPIRAL

With Col-A make 4 ch, join with ss to form ring.

Round 1a: continuing with Col-A, work 3 ch, 4–6 tr (US dc) into ring, pull long loop on hook and remove hook, drop Col-A.

Round 1b: bring in Col-B, work 3 ch, 4–6 tr (US dc) into same ring, work tr (US dc) into each ch of Col-A beginning ch, then work tr (US dc) into each tr (US dc) of Col-A (remember to increase appropriately and keep work flat) until sts run out, pull up a long loop on your hook, remove hook, drop Col-B.

Round 2: pick up Col-A, work tr (US dc) into each ch of Col-B beginning ch, then work tr (US dc) into each tr (US dc) of Col-B (remember to increase appropriately and keep work flat) until sts run out, pull up a long loop on hook, remove hook, drop Col-A, go back to Col-B.

Go back and forth between the colours to desired size.

Don't be limited by the two colours suggested in these instructions. Try three or more colours, as in the second photo; vary the rounds by working in dc (US sc), htr (US hdc) or bullions, or work out other combinations like mixing bullions and trebles. Detailed instructions for working bullions are given in the next chapter.

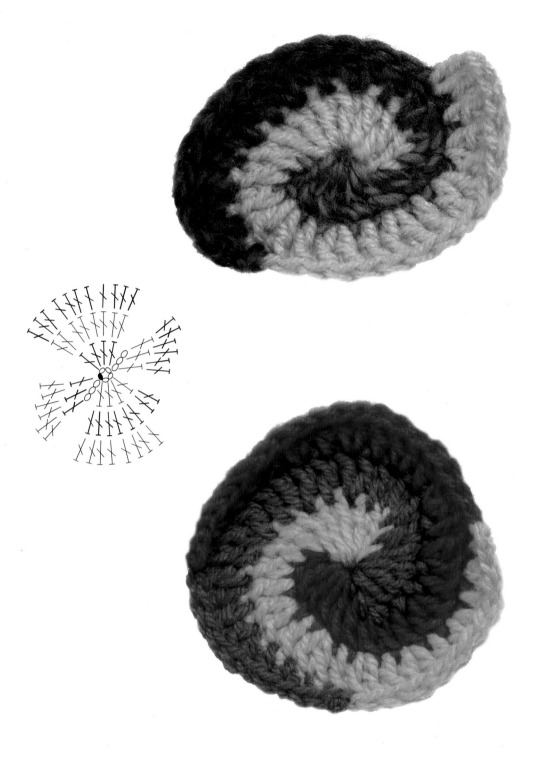

DOUBLE CIRCLE

Use contrasting textured yarns for each circle, for example, smooth centre, mohair outer. You can also substitute tr (US dc) for htr (US hdc) or dc (US sc) alternately for the first and second circle.

1st Circle: 3 ch, join with ss to form a ring, 3 ch, into ring work 12 tr (US dc), join with ss to first tr (US dc), finish off. Depending on the yarn you use, you may have to increase or decrease the number of tr (US dc).

2nd Circle: join in new yarn in any tr (US dc) of first circle, 3 ch (counts as tr [US dc]), tr (US dc) in same st, work 2 tr (US dc) in next tr and in each tr (US dc) around, join with ss to first tr (US dc). Again, depending on the yarn you use, you may have to increase or decrease the number of tr (US dc). Keep checking that your work is staying flat.

double circle

Surface embellishments

SURFACE CHAINS

These are always worked on the right side.

Surface chain 1: join yarn where needed, then work ss in a zigzag fashion across the surface of knitted/crochet piece.

Surface chain 2: join yarn where needed, 1 ch, dc (US sc) in same st, *1, 2 or 3 ch (depending on desired effect), dc (US sc) in next st, repeat from * working in zigzag fashion across surface of knitted/crochet piece.

Surface chain 3: join yarn where needed and follow outlines of pieces to enhance shapes.

CRAB STITCH

Reverse dc (US sc) is always worked on right side and in the opposite direction.

As usual join yarn where needed, 1 ch, *insert hook into the next st on right, yoh and draw up a loop, yoh and draw through both loops on hook, repeat from * to desired length.

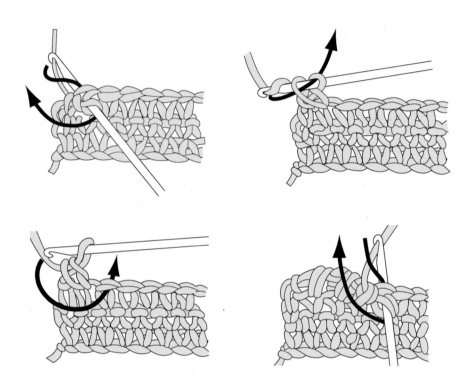

RUFFLES

Ruffles are always worked on the right side to add interest or to hide an unsightly join or a colour that you feel isn't quite right. They are best worked in finer yarns. Knitted ruffles are softer and lie flat, crochet ruffles tend to be stiffer and sit more upright. Both are effective and add a sculptural aspect to your work.

Knitted ruffle

Draw up a number of loops where needed and knit into front and back of each stitch, repeat this row at least twice.

Crochet ruffle

Join yarn where needed, 3 ch, *5 to 8 tr (US dc) in same st, repeat from * to desired length. For variations try substituting tr (US dc) for htr (US hdc) (2 ch to start) or dc (US sc) (1 ch to start).

CROCHET MESH

Mesh can be made separately or worked directly onto a starter patch. Add lengths of crochet chain, ribbon, cord, strands of yarn, etc. threaded through each space.

As separate patch

Make 14 ch.

Row 1: tr (US dc) in 6th ch from hook, *1 ch, skip next 1 ch, tr (US dc) in next ch, repeat from * to last ch.

Row 2: 4 ch (counts as 1 tr [US dc] + 1 ch sp), turn, *tr (US dc) in next tr (US dc), 1 ch, repeat from * to beginning ch, tr (US dc) in 3rd ch of beginning ch.

Repeat Row 2 to desired size.

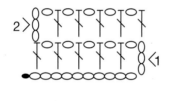 Mesh

Working directly onto starter patch

Join yarn where needed, 4 ch (counts as 1 tr [US dc] + 1 ch sp), work
(1 tr [US dc], 1 ch) evenly across the edge of patch.

JOINING PATCHES

These two diagrams are examples of ways of laying out and joining
patches. All the above patches are represented here, just as a quick
guide Use the diagrams as a starting point.

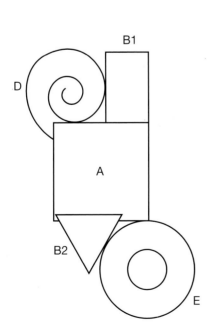

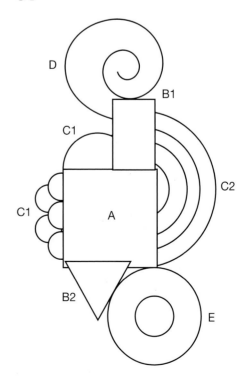

3.
Bullions galore

The crochet bullion is possibly my favourite freeform stitch, guaranteed to produce the wow effect every time over and above any other stitch I know. Bullions are beautiful, versatile, always interesting and, once mastered, relatively easy. However, crochet bullion stitch does require practice and patience when starting out. It took me many hours of practice to become proficient but it's been well worth the effort. Believe it or not, once you have mastered the technique you'll love working with bullions too.

For the beginner I suggest working directly onto a pre-made patch so that you have something to hold on to as you're working out the technique.

Variations when working directly onto fabric:

- Work along any edge varying the stitch height.

- When working scallops (see Chapter 2) substitute a round of ordinary stitches like dc (US sc) or tr (US dc) with bullions—the same applies to shells (see Chapter 2).

- Substitute ordinary stitches like dc (US sc) or tr (US dc) with bullions.

As you become more proficient, make your bullion patches separately—off a chain, in the round, odd-shaped or spiralled are but a few combination examples for you to try.

I find Tunisian hooks with their smooth shafts ideal for working bullions of all sizes. Also, though they are not absolutely necessary, 'on the roll hooks', which have a longer than usual shaft, are useful and can be purchased in any good craft store.

Tips

- Always work with right side facing.

- It is better to use smooth yarns that don't split too easily.

- When drawing through all wrapped loops, use your left thumb to separate each loop on the hook, then slip your hook under each loop until 2 remain, yoh and draw through both loops.

WORKING DIRECTLY ONTO FABRIC

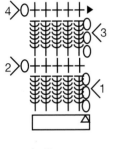

bullion on existing patch

1st Bullion: choose a straight edge on a pre-made patch and with right side facing join in yarn and make a number of ch needed for height of st (e.g. 3 ch), *wind yarn evenly around hook several times (e.g. 5 or 6)*, insert hook into same st as beginning ch, **yoh and draw up a loop (even to the height of the bullion you are about to make) and draw through all loops until 2 loops remain, yoh and draw through last 2 loops**—bullion made.

2nd and subsequent bullions: repeat from * to *, this time insert hook into st or sp close to first bullion, and repeat from ** to **.

WORKING ALONG A CHAIN

Make this bullion patch separately then join to pre-made patch, or use the motif itself as a starter patch.

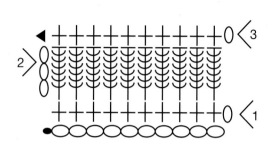 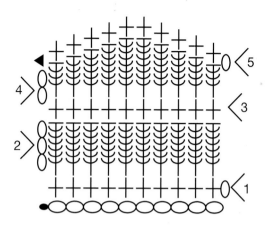

Make the number of ch required for length of patch plus one (e.g. 10 ch + 1 ch = 11 ch).

Row 1: (wrong side) turn, dc (US sc) into 2nd ch from hook and in each ch across—10 dc (US sc).

Row 2: (right side) 3 ch, turn, work bullion st into each dc (US sc) across—10 bullions.

Row 3: (wrong side) 1 ch, turn, dc (US sc) in each bullions st across—10 dc (US sc).

Repeat Rows 2 and 3 to desired size.

Any number of rows can be made in this way. Try changing colours and textures (uniformly or randomly), or work a number of trebles and bullions (e.g. 2 tr [US dc], 2 bullions) in a row for variation.

Bullions in the round

Make these bullions separately and join with a slip seam (see special instruction in Chapter 2) to a pre-made patch, to fill an appropriate size space, or use the motif itself as a starter patch.

BULLION IN THE ROUND 1

3 ch, join with ss to form a ring, 3 ch (or number required for bullion height), work as many bullions as required to keep motif flat, join with ss to the first bullion (skipping beginning 3 ch).

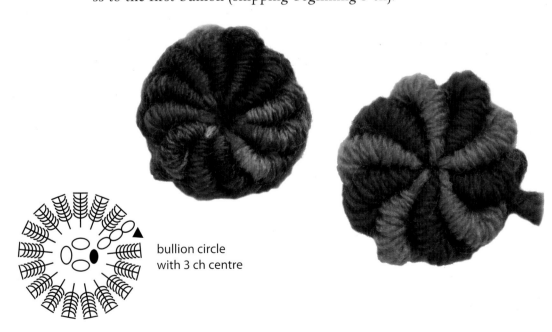

bullion circle
with 3 ch centre

bullion & tr circle
with 3 ch centre

Variations

- Alternate the colours (two or more) for each bullion.

- Use a mixture of trebles and bullions, for example, textured tr (US dc), smooth bullion.

BULLION IN THE ROUND 2

3 ch, join with ss to form a ring.

Round 1: 1 ch, work 8 dc (US sc) into ring.

Round 2: 3 ch (or number required for bullion height), work 2 bullions into each dc (US sc) around, join with ss in first bullion (skipping beginning 3 ch).

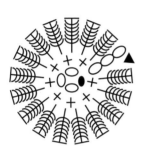

bullion circle
with dc centre

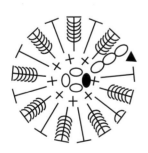

bullion & tr circle
with dc centre

Variations

- Finish off after Round 1 and change colour for Round 2.

- Use tr (US dc) or htr (US hdc) in round 1 instead of dc (US sc).

- Alternate the colours in Round 2, for example, one black, one white.

- Use a combination of trebles and bullions, for example, textured tr (US dc), smooth bullion.

Odd-shaped bullions

Use your imagination here, for the possibilities are endless.

OVAL BULLIONS

Make a number of ch, dc (US sc) in 2nd ch from hook and in each ch to last ch, 3 dc (US sc) in last ch.

Continue by working the unused loops of the row just made, working dc (US sc) in each loop to last unused loop, 2 more dc (US sc) in unused loop of first dc (US sc), join with ss to first dc (US sc), 3 ch, work bullions into each dc (US sc) around, remembering to allow for the turn by working extra bullions in the end dc (US sc) on each side.

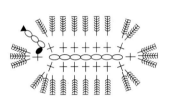

odd shaped bullion 1

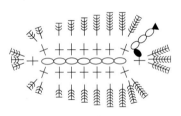

odd shaped bullion 2

Variations

- ▫ Change colour for centre.

- ▫ Alternate colours for each bullion.

- ▫ Taper the bullion size, for example, start with a 3-wrap bullion and increase to 8 to 10 wraps to the turn, then taper back down to 3 wraps on the other side.

SPIRAL BULLIONS

Take your time with these, be patient. You can achieve some wonderful nautilus shell shapes.

Colour 1: 3 ch, join with ss to form a ring, 1 ch, work 8 dc (US sc) into ring (it's a good idea to mark the first of the 8 dc [US sc] with a short piece of yarn), do not join, pull up a long loop and drop Col-1.

Colour 2: in sp before first dc (US sc) join in Col-2, 2 ch, work 2 x 3-wrap bullions in first dc (US sc), 2 x 4-wrap bullions in next dc (US sc), 2 x 5-wrap bullions and so on until 2 x 10-wrap bullions have been worked around to Col-1, pull up a long loop and drop Col-2.

Colour 1: pick up Col-1, dc (US sc) in each of first 2 ch of colour 2, then work 2 dc (US sc) in each bullion around, pull up a long loop and drop Col-1.

Colour 2: pick up Col-2 and work 1 x 11-wrap bullion in each of the next 2 single dc (US sc), then continue with 2 x 12-wrap bullions in next dc (US sc), 1 x 13-wrap bullion in next dc (US sc), 1 x 13-wrap and 1 x 14-wrap bullion in next dc (US sc), finish off.

Colour 1: pick up Col-1, work 2 dc (US sc) in each bullion around to end, finish off.

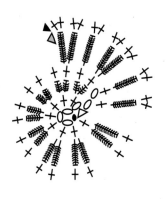

A 14-wrap bullion is enough to produce a good size spiral, however, you can continue increasing the wraps following the above pattern until you reach the size and shape you desire.

BENT BULLIONS

These can be made as a starter patch or worked around the edge or across the face of an existing patch.

Bent bullion starter patch

Make 11 ch or other uneven number of ch.

Row 1: (right side) dc (US sc) in 2nd ch from hook and in each ch across—10 dc (US sc).

Row 2: 1 ch, turn, dc (US sc) in first st and in each st across—10 dc (US sc).

Row 3: 1 ch turn, dc (US sc) in first 2 sts, *work bent bullion st, dc (US sc) in next 2 sts, repeat from * across to last st, dc (US sc) in last st—3 x bent bullion sts.

Row 4: 1 ch, turn, dc (US sc) in first st and in each st across—10 dc (US sc).

Row 5: 1 ch turn, dc (US sc) in first st, *work bent bullion st, dc (US sc) in next 2 sts, repeat from * across—3 x bent bullion sts.

Row 6: 1 ch, turn, dc (US sc) in first st and in each st across, finish off—10 dc (US sc).

BENT BULLION STITCH

Evenly wind yarn around hook 15 times, insert hook into next st and draw up a loop (even to height of bullion about to be made) and draw through all loops on hook until 2 loops remain, yoh and draw through last 2 loops, dc (US sc) in next st—bent bullion st made.

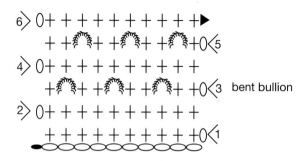

bent bullion

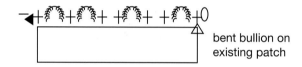

bent bullion on existing patch

Quick bullion tutorial

Part 1: make any number of ch plus 3, *wrap yarn around hook shaft 3 times—4 loops on hook.

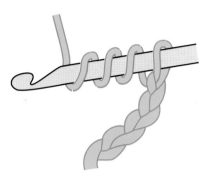

Part 2: insert hook into 4th ch from hook and draw up a loop—5 loops on hook.

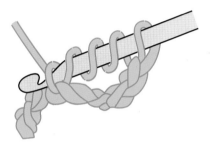

Part 3: draw this loop just made through the 3-wrap loops only—2 loops left on hook.

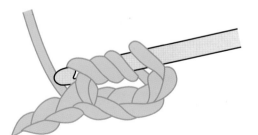 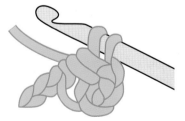

Drawing through all the wraps is the most difficult part when mastering bullions. You can either:

- Draw through one wrapped loop at a time by using your left thumb to separate each loop on hook then slipping your hook under each loop until 2 loops remain.

- Lift off each loop manually with your fingers until 2 loops remain.

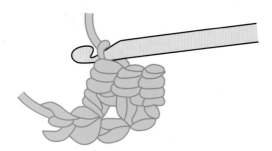

Part 4: yoh and draw through both loops—1 loop on hook, bullion made.

For subsequent bullions repeat from * in Part 1, inserting hook into next ch.

Gallery A

BAGS, BAGS, BAGS ...

Acacia (top left), **Banksia 3** (above) and **Coral** (left) feature masses of tiny glass beads which were sewn to the freeform fabrics before they were attached to the bags' shade-cloth bases. All have a satin lining. Acacia has wooden ring handles, Banksia a simple crochet handle, and Coral a novelty handle.

Spirals (right), a bag with night-time coral reef colours, was finished with hand-painted wooden handles and couched lengths of beads. Large spirals interwoven with bullions make up the fabric. Spirals has a satin-lined shade-cloth base, and is highlighted with hand-painted wooden rod handles and couched lengths of hand-painted wooden beads.

Left: **Mardi Gras** has lots of ruffles, spirals and scallops worked in outrageously bright novelty yarns attached to a rectangular shade-cloth base. A satin lining, hand-painted wooden bead tassels and a simple crochet handle form the finishing touches.

Merlot Round and spiral bullions worked around a strip of basic Tunisian crochet make up the freeform fabric attached to the shaped shade-cloth base. A satin lining, hand-painted wooden ring handle and brass buttons complete this piece.

Left: **Carnival** features every variegated yarn I could lay my hands on to make up the freeform fabric, which was attached to a round shade-cloth base with a basic Tunisian crochet gusset. The bag was given a satin lining and a simple crochet handle.

Wild Berry A wet felted pouch adorned with embedded bullion motifs, Vilene patches and overcast running stitch evolved into this little purse, which was completed with a satin lining, hand-painted wooden beads and a simple crochet handle.

Felt tassel The bag base, complete with handle, was crocheted in trebles (US double crochet) then felted in the washing machine. The tassels, made separately, were dry felted to the finished bag.

Autumn Glow For this bag, wet felted, freeform and Vilene patches were welded together with the dry felting method then attached to the shaped shade-cloth base. The bag was completed with a satin lining and a wooden handle.

Rock Pool features freeform patches built around wet felted patches edged with blanket stitch. The freeform fabric was attached to a rectangular shade-cloth base which was satin lined. A hand-painted wooden handle and highlights of novelty fake hand-painted shells and starfish add to the fun.

For these two little cuties I attached freeform fabric to existing bags.

4.
Novelty patches

Use the following patch patterns to bring even more interest and, in many cases, sculptural effects to your work. They are another quick and easy way to achieve that *wow* effect, and while some of the stitches may require a little more concentration than others, all of them will become wonderful additions to your overall crochet repertoire. Don't be limited by my suggestions—you may even have some novelty stitches of your own. Be daring, experiment.

Crochet wings (lazy J stitch)

These are made separately and attached when complete.

Make 8 ch.

Row 1: dc (US sc) in 3rd ch from hook (place marker in this 2-ch sp), 2 dc (US sc) in next ch, 1 htr (US hdc) in next ch, 2 htr (US hdc) in next ch, 1 tr (US dc) in next ch, 2 tr (US dc) in last ch; do not turn.

Row 2: using front loops of Row 1 only, 1 ch, then work crab st (reverse dc [US sc]) in each st to end, ss into first 2-ch sp; do not turn.

Row 3: 1 ch, then using unused loops behind crab st work 1 dc (US sc) in first st, 2 dc (US sc) in next st, 1 htr (US hdc) in next st, 2 htr (US hdc) in next st, 1 tr (US dc) in next st, 2 tr (US dc) in next st, leave last 3 loops unused; do not turn.

Row 4: repeat Row 2.

Repeat Rows 3 and 4 three more times. Finish off.

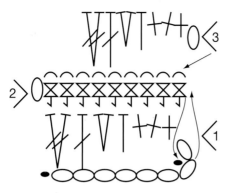

work in unused
loops of row 2

Fairy wing

Variations

- Make more or less rows for larger or smaller wings.

- Work each row in a different colour.

- Work crab st only in a different colour (remember to carry back and work over each colour alternately).

Crochet popcorns

Popcorns are worked directly onto a pre-made patch. Use them to fill in small holes, to add detail with special yarns, or in rows to make a firm edge.

Method 1: on an edge and with wrong side facing join yarn, work 3 to 5 (or more) incomplete tr (US dc) in same place as join, yoh and draw through all loops on hook, pull tight, turn work to right side then dc (US sc) or ss at base of join, pull tight. Finish off. Weave in ends.

Method 2: with right side facing (anywhere on patch) work popcorn as above but finish off with 1 ch when all loops drawn through, leaving a long end; draw this end and beginning tail to wrong side and tie off with a knot. Weave in ends.

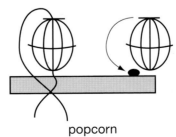

popcorn

Crochet domes

Domes are worked separately then slip seam (see special instruction in Chapter 2) to pre-made patch or to fill an appropriate size space in fabric.

Make 4 ch, work 5 to 8 tr (US dc) into 4th ch from hook, ss into first tr (US dc), pull tight. Finish off *or* slip seam to other domes or directly onto fabric.

Variations

- Use two strands of different yarns together.

- Make each tr (US dc) a different colour (remember to bring in new yarn when you have 2 loops on hook).

- Make clusters of domes using different yarns and colours and varying the hook size.

- Use domes upside down for a cup effect.

Corkscrews

Corkscrews can be used at edges for added interest, incorporated into the fabric or rolled up and stitched to form a flower and attached where required. Experiment with these using different numbers of dc (US sc), htr (US hdc) or tr (US dc).

Leaving a long tail make 25 ch, 3 dc (US sc) in 2nd ch from hook, 3 dc (US sc) in next ch and in each ch to end. Finish off, tying ends into a knot.

corkscrew

Mini spiral

These are useful for adding interest to a patch that somehow doesn't have enough oomph. I even use them sometimes to fill in tiny holes.

Bring in yarn where required on base fabric, 1 ch, dc (US sc) in same st, working off dc (US sc) just made make 5 ch, then work 3 dc (US sc) in 2nd ch from hook and 3 dc (US sc) in each next 3 ch, ss to first dc (US sc). Finish off.

mini spiral

Twisted cable

This patch is useful for filling narrow gaps. You can also make an extra long cable and wind it haphazardly over your template, making it a base from which your fabric can grow.

The pattern as given is for three colours, but it can of course be made in just one colour.

With Col A make 5 ch.

Row 1: dc (US sc) in 2nd ch from hook and in each ch across—4 dc (US sc).

Row 2: 1 ch, turn, dc (US sc) in each dc (US sc) across—4 dc (US sc).

Row 3: (change to new Col when 2 loops of working st remain on hook) 1 ch, turn, work dc (US sc) in first dc (US sc), change to Col B, skip next dc (US sc), work tr (US dc) around post of dc (US sc) directly below next st on Row 1, change to Col C, work tr (US dc) around post of dc (US sc) directly below skipped st on Row 1, change to Col A, work dc (US sc) in last dc (US sc).

Row 4: with Col A repeat Row 2.

Row 5: 1 ch, turn, work dc (US sc) in first dc (US sc), change to Col C, skip next dc (US sc), work tr (US dc) around post of tr (US dc) directly below next st on Row 3, change to Col B, work tr (US dc) around post of tr (US dc) directly below skipped st on Row 3, change back to Col A, work dc (US sc) in last dc (US sc).

Row 6: with Col A repeat Row 2.

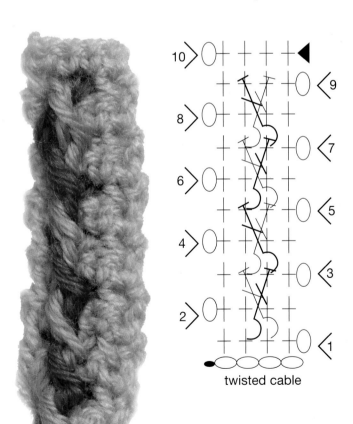

twisted cable

Row 7: 1 ch, turn, work dc (US sc) in first dc (US sc), change to Col B, skip next dc (US sc), work tr (US dc) around post of dc (US sc) directly below next st on Row 1, change to Col C, work tr (US dc) around post of dc (US sc) directly below skipped st on Row 1, change back to Col A, work dc (US sc) in last dc (US sc).

Repeat Rows 4 to 7 to desired size, ending with Row 2. Finish off.

OFFSET PUFF STITCH

In this patch a 9-loop puff st is worked around the post of tr (US dc) just made.

Make 15 ch.

Round 1: tr (US dc) in 4th ch from hook, work offset puff st around tr (US dc) just made (9 loops on hook), insert hook into next ch and draw yarn through ch and 9 loops, *1 ch, tr (US dc) into next ch, from here work offset puff st (the 9 loops) around tr (US dc) just made and back thread of previous offset puff st, repeat from * to last ch, do not finish off, do not turn—6 x offset puff sts.

Round 2: 1 ch, work 7 dc (US sc) around back thread of previous offset puff st, work dc (US sc) into each ch of foundation ch to beginning 3 ch, work 7 dc (US sc) around beginning ch, work dc (US sc) into each offset puff st and ch to end, join with ss to first dc (US sc). Finish off or go to Round 3.

Round 3: (only if desired) 1 ch, dc (US sc) in same st, dc (US sc) in each dc (US sc) around. Finish off.

Offset puff stitch also makes a decorative bag handle, although I must advise working tightly to avoid too much stretch. Make a chain in multiples of 2 + 3 ch, then work as above.

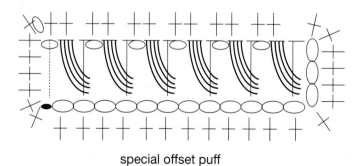

special offset puff

Special offset puff stitch

This stitch is worked directly onto a patch already made.

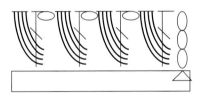

special offset puff

Basic Tunisian crochet

These instructions are for two colours, but of course apply to one colour if that is what you prefer.

With Col A make 9 ch.

Row 1: draw up a loop in 2nd ch from hook and in each ch across—9 loops on hook.

Row 2: drop Col A and bring in Col B, *yoh and draw through 2 loops (one of each Col), repeat from * across until one loop remains.

Row 3: continuing with Col B, draw up a loop in 2nd vertical bar from hook and in each vertical bar across—9 loops on hook.

Row 4: drop Col B and pick up Col A, *yoh and draw through 2 loops (one of each Col), repeat from * across until one loop remains.

Row 5: continuing with Col A, draw up a loop in 2nd vertical bar from hook and in each vertical bar across—9 loops on hook.

Repeat Rows 2 to 5 to desired size, ending with a pick-up row (Row 2 or 4), dc (US sc) or ss in each vertical bar across, finish off.

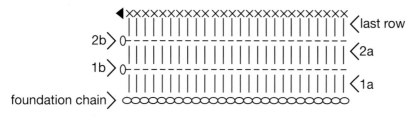

tunisian knit stitch

Cobble stitch

Take care in working this pattern that the cobbles do not sit on top of each other.

These instructions are for two colours, but of course apply to one colour if that is what you prefer.

With Col A make 9 ch.

Row 1: draw up a loop in 2nd ch from hook and in each ch across—9 loops on hook.

Row 2: drop Col A and bring in Col B (count as first loop), yoh and draw through 2 loops (one of each Col), 3 ch, *yoh and draw through 2 loops (one of each Col) twice, 3 ch, repeat from * across until one loop remains—4 x 3ch groups.

Row 3: (work behind 3ch groups) continuing with Col B, draw up a loop in 2nd vertical bar from hook and in each vertical bar across—9 loops on hook—4 x cobbles.

Row 4: drop Col B and pick up Col A, 3 ch, *yoh and draw through 2 loops (one of each Col) twice, 3 ch, repeat from * across until one loop remains—4 x 3ch groups.

Row 5: (work behind 3 ch groups) continuing with Col A, draw up a loop in 2nd vertical bar from hook and in each vertical bar across—9 loops on hook—4 x cobbles.

Repeat Rows 2 to 5 to desired size ending with a pick-up row (Row 2 or 4), dc (US sc) or ss in each vertical bar across. Finish off.

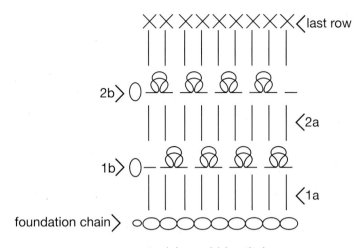

2b⟩

2a

1b⟩

1a

foundation chain⟩

tunisian cobble stitch

Limpet (winding) stitch

For the best results with this stitch, use smooth and/or shiny yarns.

Limpet stitch on existing patch

On an existing patch bring in yarn and make a number of dc (US sc) (say 3), *cast on 7 new loops onto hook as follows: working hook (yoh) in an anti-clockwise direction, pick up yarn and draw under and through 7 times (8 loops on hook), yoh and draw through all 8 loops, 1 ch to close, dc (US sc) into next stitch to anchor the limpet, make a number of dc (US sc) (say 2) and repeat from *.

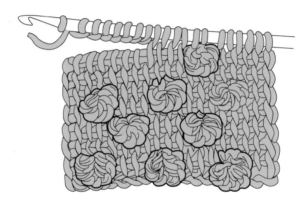

Showing limpet stitch incorporated into a basic background of basic Tunisian crochet to make a separate patch.

Limpet stitch as starter patch

Limpets can also be incorporated into a basic background of dc (US sc)
to make a separate patch.

Make 11 ch.

Row 1: dc (US sc) in 2nd ch from hook and in each ch across—10 dc
(US sc).

Row 2: 1 ch, turn, dc (US sc) in first and each st across—10 dc (US sc).

Row 3: 1 ch, turn, dc (US sc) in first 2 sts, *work limpet st, dc (US sc) in
next 3 sts, repeat from across to last 2 sts, dc (US sc) in last 2 sts—10 dc
(US sc)—3 x limpets.

Row 4: 1 ch, turn, dc (US sc) in first and each st across—10 dc (US sc).

Row 5: 1 ch, turn, dc (US sc) in first 3 sts, *work limpet st, dc (US sc) in
next 3 sts, repeat from across to last 4 sts, dc (US sc) in last 4 sts—10 dc
(US sc)—2 x limpets.

Row 6: 1 ch, turn, dc (US sc) in first and each st across—10 dc (US sc).

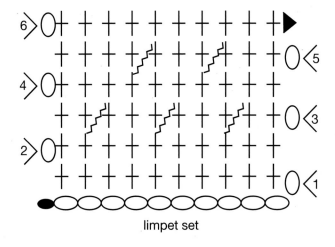

limpet set

Coil stitch

Coil stitch can be worked along an edge or as a surface embellishment on an existing patch.

Bring in yarn where required on base fabric, anchor with ss, *3 ch, skip 2 sts (or space equivalent to where 2 sts might be), ss in next st, 1 ch, turn (wrong side will be facing), work 5 dc (US sc) over 3ch loop, turn (right side will be facing), dc (US sc) in next 2 sts (or space equivalent to where 2 sts might be), repeat from * as many times as required, anchor with ss to finish off.

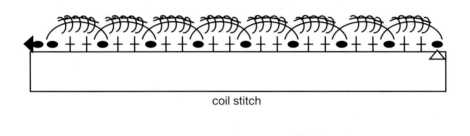

coil stitch

row direction > +++++ < stitch direction

Medallion stitch

Another stitch to embellish a pre-made patch.

Round 1: bring in yarn where required on base fabric, anchor with ss, *3 ch, anchor with ss 3 rows below (or space equivalent to where 3 rows might be), 3 ch, anchor with ss in st next on working row (or space equivalent to where next st might be)—2 x 3ch loops.

Round 2: working around 3ch loops just made, make 7 tr (US dc) around post of each of the two 3ch loops, anchor with ss to first ss, finish off.

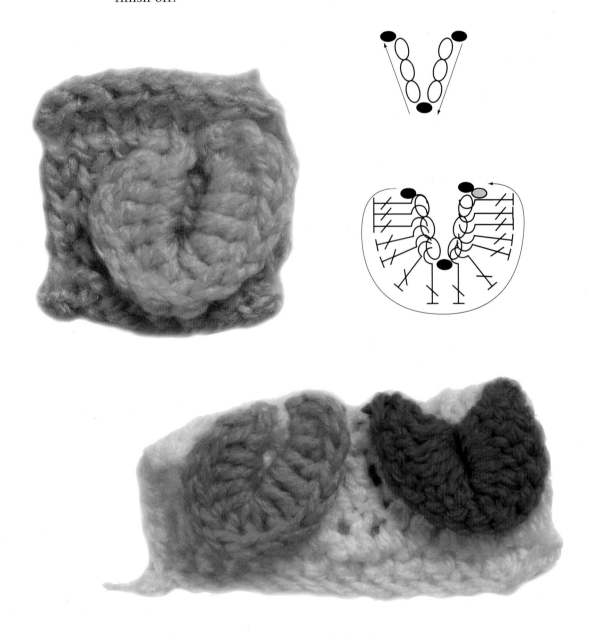

Gallery B
HEADWEAR: FUN, FANTASTIC, OUT THERE ...

Forest Nymph (left) and **Autumn** (bottom)
I used a commercial dressmaking hat pattern for the basic shape of these hats. The bands were worked in double crochet (US single crochet) and tassels added to the crowns for extra fun.

This **Turkish Hat** is kiddie-size, but the 9 cm (3 ½ in) wide freeform band can easily be made to the desired head size and the round flat crown crocheted to suit.

Blue Beret Here a large dinner plate was used as a template, and the band worked in double crochet (US single crochet).

For **Misty** and **Blue Tassel**, a 52 x 22 cm (20 ½ x 8 ½ in) rectangle folded in half to make a square was used as a template. The bands were worked in double crochet (US single crochet).

Rasta 1 started out as a bag that was never going to work no matter what I did. I turned it upside down, added the tassels—presto! Love it!!

A commercial dressmaking hat pattern was used for the head shape for these two hoods, and then I just kept adding more and more patches for the extended scarves.

Rasta 2 and **Rasta 3** The crowns were crocheted in trebles (US double crochet), then felted in the washing machine. The bands were crocheted directly onto the crowns in double crochet (US single crochet), and the tassels, made separately, were then sewn to the finished beanies.

Rasta 4 The whole beanie was worked in double crochet (US single crochet) using only three different yarns. Hand-painted wooden bead tassels, ponytail tassels and simple couching stitch embroidery add the finishing touches.

5.
Floral elements ...
and stars

Although many of the following motif patterns, most of them made separately and sewn in later, are quite similar, the smallest variation will add extra interest to your work. Experiment with stitches, yarns and hook sizes.

Flower 1

Leaving a long tail end to sew in place later, make 4 ch and join with ss to form ring.

Round 1: 1 ch, into ring work 10 dc (US sc), join with ss to first dc (US sc)—10 dc (US sc).

Round 2: *3 ch, 4 tr (US dc) in same st, ss in next 2 sts, repeat from * around, finish off—5 petals made.

Variations

▫ Work Rounds 1 and 2 in different colours.

▫ Work Round 2 in back loops only.

▫ Embellish unused loops using a finer or contrasting thread or yarn and working dc (US sc) or (ss, 1 ch) in each unused loop around.

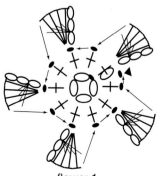

flower 1

Flower 2

Leaving a long tail end to sew in place, later make 5 ch and join with ss to form ring.

Round 1: 3 ch (counts as tr [US dc]), work 3 tr (US dc) into ring, 3 ch, turn, tr (US dc) in first and each st across (5 tr [US dc] petal made), 3 ch, turn, *working across and behind petal just made work 4 tr (US dc) into ring, 3 ch, turn, tr (US dc) in first and each st across, 3 ch, turn, repeat from * 6 times more, join with ss to 3rd ch of beginning 3ch, finish off—8 petals made.

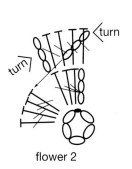

flower 2

Flower 3

Leaving a long tail end to sew in place later, make 5 ch and join with ss to form ring.

Round 1: 3 ch (count as tr [US dc] [beginning ch]), 2 tr (US dc) into ring, 6 ch, ss around post of last tr (US dc) made, *3 tr (US dc) into ring, 6 ch, ss around post of last tr (US dc) made, repeat from * 6 more times, join with ss to 3rd ch of beginning 3ch—8 x 6ch loops.

Round 2: ss into next tr (US dc), *12 tr (US dc) in next 6ch loop, ss into 2nd tr (US dc) of next 3 tr (US dc) group, repeat from * 7 times more, join with ss to first ss, finish off—8 petals.

Variation

▫ Work Rounds 1 and 2 in different colours.

Flower 4

Leaving a long tail end to sew in place later, make 5 ch and join with ss to form ring.

Round 1: 3 ch (count as tr [US dc] [beginning ch]), 2 tr (US dc) into ring, 6 ch, ss around post of last tr (US dc) made, *3 tr (US dc) into ring, ss around post of last tr (US dc) made, repeat from * 6 more times, join with ss to 3rd ch of beginning 3ch—8 x 6ch loops.

Round 2: ss into next tr (US dc), *work (2 dc [US sc], 2 htr [US hdc], 4 tr [US dc], 2 htr [US hdc], 2 dc [US sc]) in next 6ch loop, ss into 2nd tr (US dc) of next 3 tr (US dc) group, repeat from * 7 times more, join with ss to first ss, finish off—8 petals.

Variation

▫ Work Rounds 1 and 2 in different colours.

Flower 5

Leaving a long tail end to sew in place later, make 2 ch.

Round 1: 5 dc (US sc) in 2nd ch from hook, join with ss to first dc (US sc)—5 dc (US sc).

Round 2: (first petal) 3 ch, then work (cluster, 3 ch, ss) in same st, (last 4 petals) work (ss, 3 ch, cluster, 3 ch, ss) in next st, join with ss in base of beginning 3ch, finish off—5 petals.

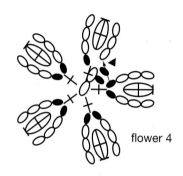

flower 4

CLUSTER

 (yoh, insert hook into st indicated and draw up a loop, yoh and draw through 2 loops) 3 times in same st, yoh and draw through 4 loops on hook—cluster made.

Flower 6 (daisy)

This flower is made in two parts, first the petals, then the centre dome which is attached to the patch.

Petals

Leaving a long tail end to sew in place later, make 5 ch and join with ss to form ring.

Round 1: 1 ch, 10 dc (US sc) into ring, join with ss to first dc (US sc)—10 dc (US sc).

Round 2: *8 ch, ss in 2nd ch from hook, dc (US sc) in next ch, htr (US hdc) in last 5 ch, ss into next st on Round 1, repeat from * around, finish off—10 petals.

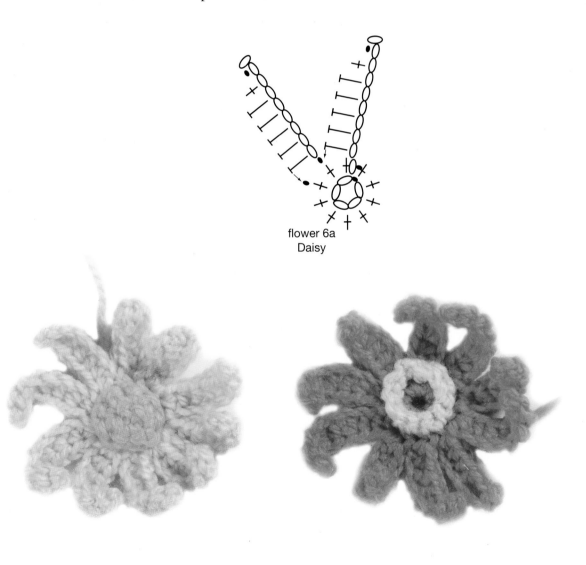

flower 6a
Daisy

Centre dome

Round 1: 2 ch, 4 dc (US sc) into 2nd ch from hook, join with ss to first dc (US sc)—4 dc (US sc).

Round 2: 1 ch, 2 dc (US sc) in each st around, join with ss to first dc (US sc), finish off, leaving a long tail end to sew in place in centre of petals—8 dc (US sc).

flower 6b
Daisy centre dome

Variation

▫ Work Round 1 of petals pattern as above. On Round 2 work in back loops only, then with a fine yarn embellish unused loops as desired.

Flower 7 (bluebell)

Leaving a long tail end to sew in place later, make 2 ch.

Round 1: 6 dc (US sc) into 2nd ch from hook, do not join, place marker—6 dc (US sc).

Round 2: 2 dc (US sc) in each st around to marker, do not join—12 dc (US sc).

Rounds 3 and 4: dc (US sc) in each st around to marker, do not join—12 dc (US sc).

Round 5: (work in front loops only) *4 dc (US sc) in next front loop, ss in next front loop, repeat from * around, join with ss to first st, finish off—6 x petals. Weave in tail end and sew a bead in centre of bluebell.

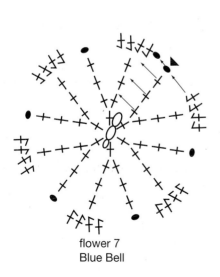

flower 7
Blue Bell

Flower 8

Leaving a long tail end to sew in place later, make 5 ch and join with ss to form ring.

Round 1: 1 ch, work (dc (US sc), 6 ch) into ring 8 times, join with ss to first st—8 x 6ch loops.

Round 2: (work behind 6-ch loops of Round 1) 2 ch, work (ss, 2 ch) in next dc (US sc) 7 times, join with ss in first st—8 x 2ch loops.

First petal: from now on you will be working in rows radiating out from centre.

Row 1: *ss into next 2ch loop, 1 ch, 4 dc (US sc) in same loop—4 dc (US sc).

Row 2: 1 ch, turn, 2 dc (US sc) in first st, dc (US sc) in each next 2 sts, 2 dc (US sc) in last st—6 dc (US sc).

Rows 3 and 4: 1 ch, turn, dc (US sc) in each st across—6 dc (US sc).

Row 5: 1 ch, turn, dc (US sc) in first 5 sts, leave last st unused—5 dc (US sc).

Row 6: 1 ch, turn, dc (US sc) in first 4 sts, leave last st unused—4 dc (US sc).

Row 7: 1 ch, turn, dc (US sc) in first 3 sts, leave last st unused—3 dc (US sc).

Row 8: 1 ch, turn, dc (US sc) in first 2 sts, leave last st unused—2 dc (US sc).

Row 9: 1 ch, turn, dc (US sc) in first sts, ss in last st—1 dc (US sc) and 1 ss.

Row 10: (omit if a flat petal preferred) work ss in each row down side of petal to 2ch loop, ss in 2ch loop (this last step will make the petal curl).

Subsequent petals: repeat from *7 times more, join with ss to first ss, finish off.

Variations

- Work the centre in a different colour.

- Use a variegated yarn for petals.

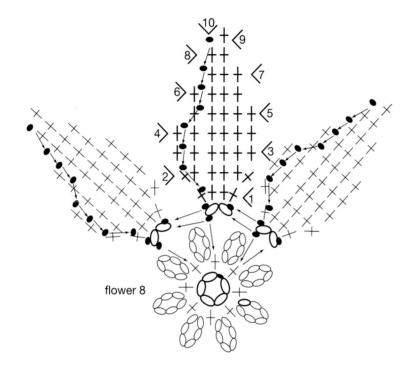

flower 8

Flower 9 (poppy)

Petals

Leaving a long tail end to sew in place later, make 5 ch and join with ss to form ring.

Round 1: 1 ch, into ring work (dc [US sc], 6 ch) 5 times, join with ss to fist dc (US sc)—5 x 6ch loops.

Round 2: *ss into next 6ch loop, work (4 ch, 10 dtr [US tr], 4 ch, ss) in same loop, repeat from * 4 times more, join with ss in first ss—5 half-petals.

Round 3: *working up along side of next petal, ss in each next 4 ch, 3 ch, tr (US dc) in each next 10 dtr (US tr), 3 ch, working down along side of same petal ss in each next 4 ch, repeat from * 4 times more, join with ss in first ss, finish off—5 complete petals.

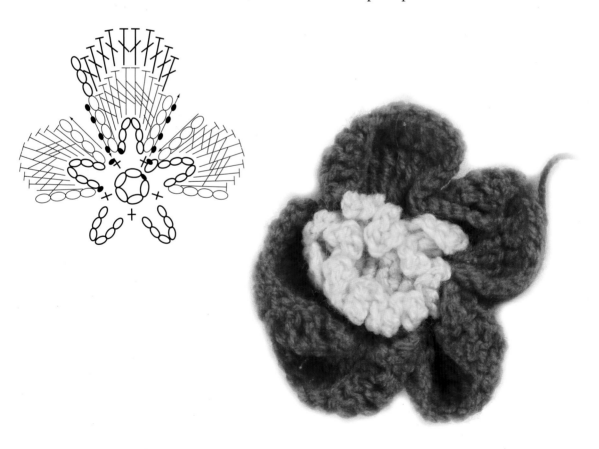

Centre

Leaving a long tail end to sew in place later, make 2 ch.

Round 1: 6 dc (US sc) in 2nd ch from hook, join with ss in first dc (US sc)—6 dc (US sc).

Round 2: 1 ch, 2 dc (US sc) in first and each st around, join with ss in first dc (US sc)—12 dc (US sc).

Round 3: 8 ch, in next st work (ss, 8 ch) 11 times, join with ss in first ss, finish off—12 x 8ch loops. Attach to centre of petals.

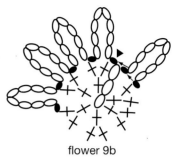

flower 9b

Flower 10 (sunflower)

Petals

Leaving a long tail end to sew in place later, make 4 ch and join with ss to form ring.

Round 1: 3 ch (count as tr [US dc]), 11 tr (US dc) into ring, join with ss to top of beginning 3ch—12 tr (US dc).

Round 2: *10 ch, ss in 2nd ch from hook and in next 2 ch, dc (US sc) in last 6 ch, ss into next st on Round 1, repeat from * around, finish off—12 petals.

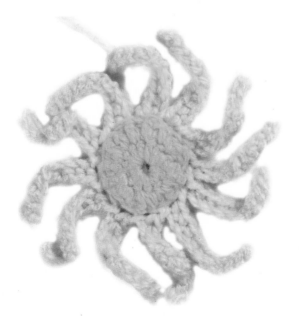

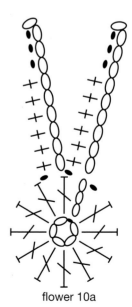

flower 10a

flower 10b

Centre

Leaving a long tail end to sew in place later, make 5 ch and join with ss to form ring.

Round 1: (right side) 1 ch, 12 dc (US sc) into ring, do not join, place marker—12 dc (US sc).

Round 2: 2 dc (US sc) in next and each st around, finish off, leaving a long tail end to sew in place later—24 dc (US sc). With wrong side of centre facing, attach to centre of sunflower petals.

Flower 11 (lazy daisy)

Leaving a long tail end to sew in place later, make 6 ch and join with ss to form ring.

Round 1: *into ring work (12 ch, ss) 8 times or as many times as required.

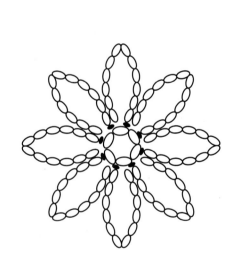

Flower 12 (spiral rose A)

This rose can be made as an embellishment to a pre-made patch, bringing in yarn where required, or made separately and sewn in place later.

Make 25 ch, do not join.

Row 1: 5 tr (US dc) in 2nd ch from hook, *ss in next ch, 5 tr (US dc) in next ch, repeat from * across, finish off leaving a long tail end, thread darning needle with tail end and take through to wrong side, drop needle.

Row 2: with right side facing, roll spiral into rose shape and using dropped needle secure rose to base fabric several times, finishing off with a bead in centre of rose.

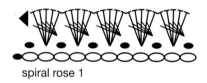

spiral rose 1

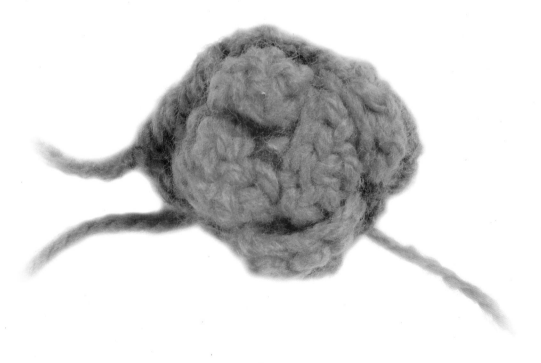

Flower 12 (spiral rose B)

This rose also can be made as an embellishment to a patch already made, bringing in yarn where required, or made separately and sewn in place later.

Make 25 ch, do not join.

Row 1: 4 tr (US dc) in 3rd ch from hook, *ss in each next 2 ch, 5 tr (US dc) in next ch, repeat from * across to last ch, ss in last ch, finish off leaving a long tail end, thread darning needle with tail end and take through to wrong side, drop needle.

Row 2: with right side facing, roll spiral into rose shape and using dropped needle secure rose to base fabric several times, finishing off with a bead in centre of rose.

spiral rose

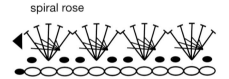

Leaf 1

Leaving a long tail end for sewing in place later, make 15 ch, do not join.

Row 1a: ss into 2nd ch from hook, dc (US sc) in each next 2 ch, htr (US hdc) in next ch, 2 htr (US hdc) in next ch, tr (US dc) in next ch, 2 tr (US dc) in next ch, tr (US dc) in next ch, dtr (US tr) in each next 2 ch, tr (US dc) in each next 2 ch, htr (US hdc) in next ch, dc (US sc) in last ch.

Row 1b: (do not turn, work in back ridge behind unused loop of foundation ch) ss in first loop, dc (US sc) in each next 2 loops, htr (US hdc) in each next 2 loops, 2 tr (US dc) in next loop, tr (US dc) in each next 2 loops, htr (US hdc) in each next 2 loops, dc (US sc) in each next 2 loops, ss in next loops, leave last loop unused. Finish off.

Variations

- Work crab st around leaf edge.

- Vary the number of sts in each ch across and around.

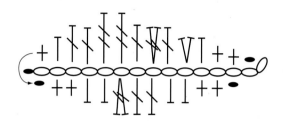

Leaf 2

Leaving a long tail end for sewing in place later, make 2 ch.

Row 1: 2 dc (US sc) in 2nd ch from hook—2 dc (US sc).

Row 2: 1 ch, turn, 2 dc (US sc) in each st across—4 dc (US sc).

Row 3: 1 ch, turn, 2 dc (US sc) in first st, dc (US sc) in each next 2 sts, 2 dc (US sc) in last st—6 dc (US sc).

Rows 4 and 5: 1 ch, turn, dc (US sc) in first and each st across—6 dc (US sc).

Row 6: 1 ch, turn, dc (US sc) in first 5 sts, leave last st unused—5 dc (US sc).

Row 7: 1 ch, turn, dc (US sc) in first 4 sts, leave last st unused—4 dc (US sc).

Row 8: 1 ch, turn, dc (US sc) in first 3 sts, leave last st unused—3 dc (US sc).

Row 9: 1 ch, turn, dc (US sc) in first 2 sts, leave last st unused—2 dc (US sc).

Row 10: 1 ch, turn, dc (US sc) in first sts, ss in last st—1 dc (US sc) and 1 ss.

Row 11: (omit this row if flat leaf preferred) work ss in each row down side of leaf to 2nd ch to beginning 2ch, ss in beginning 2ch (this last step will make the leaf curl).

Variation

▫ Work crab stitch around leaf edge.

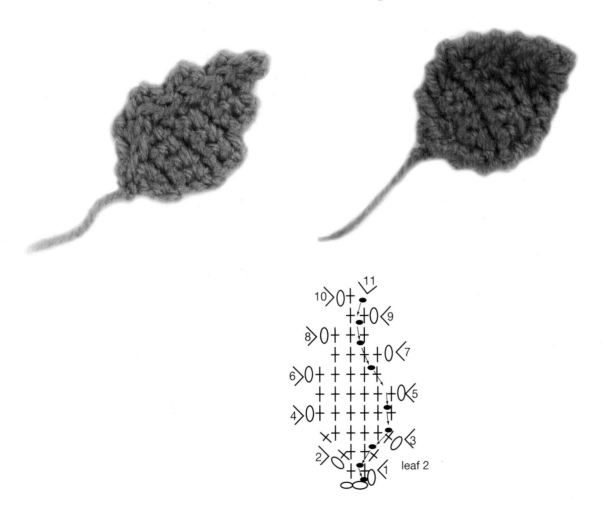

leaf 2

Gum nut

Leaving a long tail end for sewing in place later, make 2 ch.

Round 1: 6 dc (US sc) in 2nd ch from hook, do not join, place marker—6 dc (US sc)

Round 2: 2 dc (US sc) in each st around to marker, do not join, place marker—12 dc (US sc)

Round 3: dc (US sc) in each st around to marker, do not join, place marker—12 dc (US sc).

Rounds 4 to 6: repeat Round 3—12 dc (US sc).

Round 7: ss in each st around to marker, finish off leaving a long tail—12 ss.

Bring both tail ends through top of gum nut, knot or chain to form a cord.

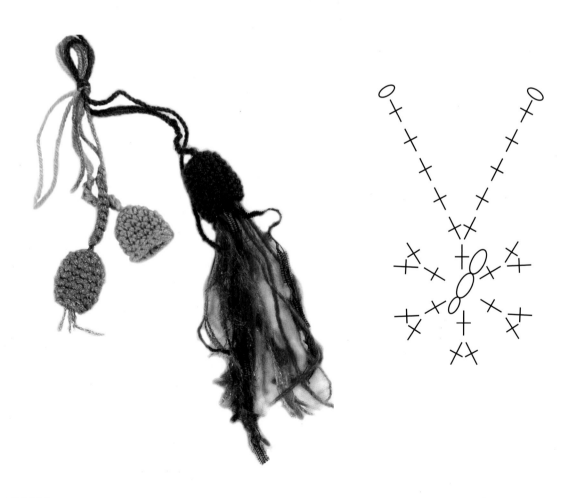

Variations

- Vary fullness of gum nut by increasing or decreasing number of sts on Round 1.

- To lengthen gum nut, repeat Round 3 to length required.

- To shorten gum nut, omit one or more of Rounds 4 to 6 as required.

Star 1

Leaving a long tail end for sewing in place later, make 3 ch and join with ss to form ring.

Round 1: *6 ch, ss in 2nd ch from hook, dc (US sc) in next ch, htr (US hdc) in next ch, tr (US dc) in each next 2 ch, dtr (US tr) in last ch, dc (US sc) into ring, repeat from * 4 times more, join with ss to base of beginning 6ch, finish off—5 point star.

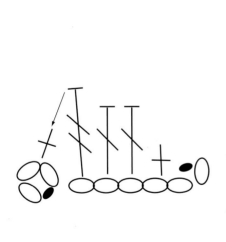

Star 2

Leaving a long tail end for sewing in place later, make 5 ch and join with ss to form ring.

Round 1: 1 ch, into ring work 16 dc (US sc), join with ss to first dc (US sc), do not finish off—16 dc (US sc).

Round 2: *5 ch, dc (US sc) in 2nd ch from hook, htr (US hdc) in next ch, tr (US dc) in next ch, dtr (US tr) in next ch, skip next 2 sts on Round 1, ss into next st, repeat from * around, join with ss to beginning st, finish off—5 point star.

Star variations

▫ Alter size and shape of both stars by increasing or decreasing number of foundation chains, then experimenting with stitches.

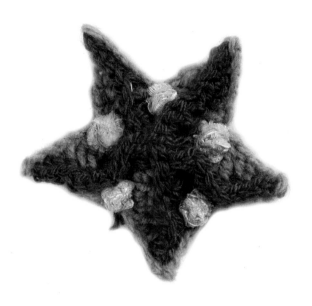

Gallery C
SCARVES AND SHRUGS AND SHAWLS

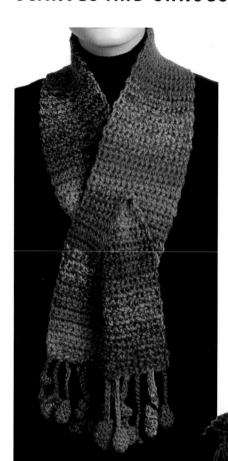

To a simple muffler (left) in double crochet (US sc) I added a few tassels—a really easy one for the beginner.

Floral Vine What to do with all those floral and leaf motifs I made for practice? Crochet a long scarf in trebles (US double crochet), sew on the motifs, work some surface chain, add a fringe and there you have it.

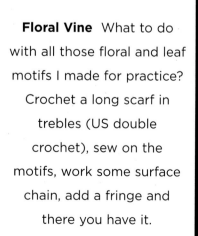

Funky Scarf Knit a thin strip, edge it with crochet mesh, thread through some novelty yarns and there you have it—another easy one for the beginner.

Winter Garden 2 Knit an extremely long scarf, bombard it with floral motifs, glass beads and tassels and you end up with an elegant showpiece.

Coralloid This unusual wrap, inspired by the colours and textures of coral reefs, incorporates beaded bullions with small knitted and crochet patches. The beaded tassels add extra weight and drape to the garment.

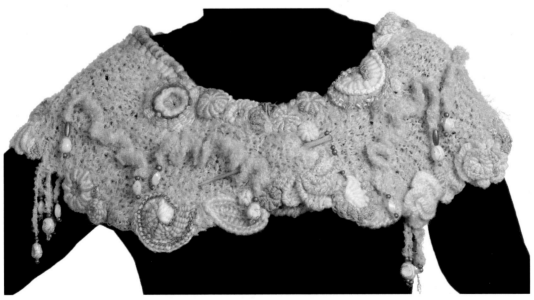

Cream Collar The inspiration for this piece came from a bygone era, and I simply brought it up to date. Start with an irregular-edged knitted collar shape, then add motifs in all the irregular spaces.

Crème Caramel Here a rectangle 56 x 48 cm (22½ x 19½ in) was used as a template, with extra patches added for the short sleeves.

Forest Inspired and **Crystal Grove** A forest reserve where I often go to find solace and inspiration influenced the colours, textures and mood for these two compositions.

Metallica utilises every metallic yarn I could find—no two motifs are the same. The square motifs were joined with varying lengths of chain, then the whole outer edge worked in trebles (US double crochet).

Spiral Web The template for this piece was a 142 x 51 cm (56 x 20 in) rectangle folded in half and joined across the top, leaving a 33 cm (13 in) neck opening at the fold. The spirals were made separately and joined together with lengths of chain. All tail ends were brought to the front and beaded with hand-made, hand-painted polymer and wooden beads.

Medea's Shawl Making this piece turned me into a bullion expert. Try making a box full of medallions yourself—every size, every variation you can think of, experiment with as many different yarns and hooks as possible and then crochet them all together with an interesting yarn.

6.
A multitude of tassels and other dangly things

Where appropriate, tassels and dangly fringes will bring a bit of razzle-dazzle to your project. A few beads here and there give a touch of glitz and glamour, plus they add weight to the tassel so it hangs better. Have lots of fun with these.

When I'm making tassels I prefer to bead as I go, threading beads onto the yarn before beginning the pattern so I'm able to bring them in where and when I like.

Where very small beads are required I use the bead-threading method illustrated in these three photos.

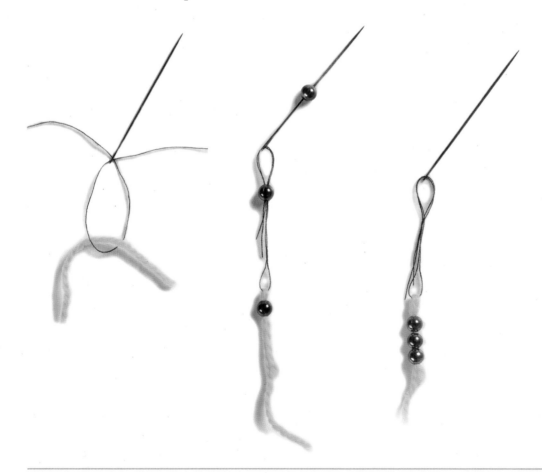

Standard single tassel

Bring together 4 to 6 of the different yarns used in your project and cut lengths appropriate to the size tassel required. With wrong side of the patch or fabric facing, insert hook into stitch or space where required and draw yarn lengths (folded in half) through stitch to form a loop, then draw all ends through loop just made. Don't be afraid to vary the size, length and thickness of tassels, to cut them off blunt or leave them raggedy—yes, all within the same project if you like.

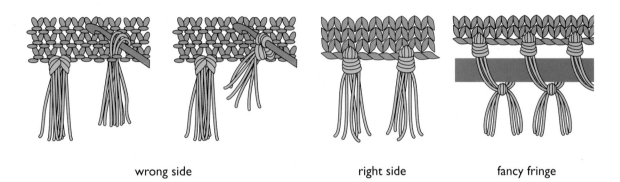

wrong side   right side   fancy fringe

Standard double tassel

The standard double tassel is worked over 5 to 7 chains depending on thickness of tassel required.

Bring in yarn where required, make 5 to 7 ch and join to patch or fabric with ss where required to form a loop; work 2 standard single tassels as above in this loop.

Note The same 5 to 7 ch loop can be used to hang any type of tassel.

tassel No. 2
standard double

Corkscrew tassel

See Chapter 4 for corkscrew pattern instructions.

To incorporate a bead at base of corkscrew, as in the central one shown here, with bead already threaded onto yarn and leaving a long tail make 25 ch or number required for length, bring up bead and ss in 2nd ch from hook, then follow corkscrew pattern as desired.

Alternatively, with a number of beads already threaded onto yarn and leaving a long tail make 25 ch or number required for length, then following corkscrew pattern bring up beads where required, as in the tassel on the right.

Hooded tassel

Hood

See Chapter 5 for the gum nut pattern instructions.

Tassel insert

Bring together 4 to 6 of the different yarns used in your project and cut lengths appropriate to the size tassel required; fold in half. Insert hook through top of gum nut and draw folded threads through the top. Using both hood tail-ends, securely tie off threads. Pull tassel down so that it sits snugly inside the hood, then knot or chain what remains of the tail ends to form a cord.

Skinny beaded tassel

Single bead tassel

With a bead already threaded onto yarn and leaving a long tail, make number of ch required for tassel length, bring up bead and ss in 2nd ch from hook then, depending on thickness of desired tassel, ss or dc (US sc) in each ch to end.

Multi bead tassel

Begin as above, and bring in more beads every 4th, 5th or 6th stitch.

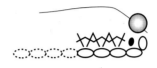

tassel No. 5

Hanging ball tassel

Make 2 ch.

Round 1: 6 dc (US sc) in 2nd ch from hook, do not join, place marker—6 dc (US sc).

Round 2: 2 dc (US sc) in each st around to marker, do not join, place marker—12 dc (US sc).

Round 3: dc (US sc) in each st around to marker, do not join, place marker—12 dc (US sc).

Round 4: *dc (US sc) dec over next 2 sts, dc (US sc) in next st, repeat from * to marker, do not join, place marker—8 dc (US sc).

Fill half-made ball with wadding or tail-end scraps, then continue with Rounds 5, 6, 7, 8.

Round 5: dc (US sc) dec over next 2 sts around to marker, do not join, place marker—4 dc (US sc).

Round 6: dc (US sc) dec over next 2 sts around to marker, do not join, place marker—2 dc (US sc).

Round 7: dc (US sc) dec over last 2 sts—1 dc (US sc).

Round 8: make number of ch required for cord length. Finish off.

DC DECREASE/DC DEC (US SC DECREASE/SC DEC)

*insert hook in next dc (US sc), yoh and pull up a loop, repeat from * for the number of sts required to decrease, draw through all loops on hook to make one st.

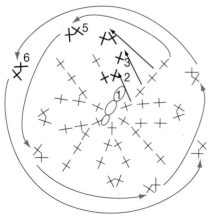

tassel No. 6a ball

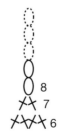

tassel No. 6b
detail round 6, 7 & 8

Offset puff clover tassel

The offset puff clover is quite a fiddly stitch but well worth the time and effort to master.

OFFSET PUFF CLOVER

Offset puff st has 4 parts and is worked loosely around 3 ch. Working around 3 ch indicated (yoh and draw up a loop from under 3 ch, yoh and draw up a loop over top of 3 ch) 9 times, yoh and draw through all loops on hook—part 1 of 4-part offset puff clover made.

Leaving a long tail make 17 ch (beginning ch) or number required for length.

Part 1: work offset puff clover (as above) around last 3 ch just made.

Part 2: 3 ch, work offset puff clover around last 3 ch just made, ss in 14th ch of beginning ch.

Part 3: 3 ch, work offset puff clover around last 3 ch just made, ss between first 2 offset puffs clover sts.

Part 4: 3 ch, work offset puff clover around last 3 ch just made, ss in 14th ch of beginning ch, 13 ch, finish off.

Twist the two 13 ch cords around each other and attach where required.

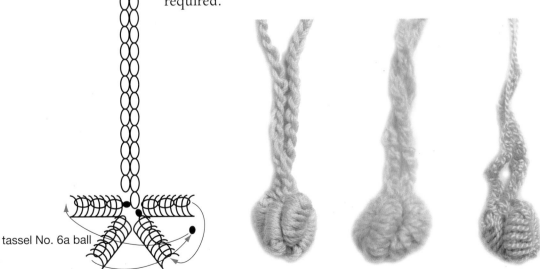

tassel No. 6a ball

Circular medallion tassel

Make 2 ch.

Round 1: 6 dc (US sc) in 2nd ch from hook, do not join, place marker—6 dc (US sc).

Round 2: 2 dc (US sc) in each st around to marker, do not join, place marker—12 dc (US sc).

Round 3: *2 dc (US sc) in next st, dc (US sc) in next st, repeat from * around to marker, do not join, place marker—18 dc (US sc).

Round 4: *2 dc (US sc) in next st, dc (US sc) in each next 2 sts, repeat from * to marker, join with ss to first st—24 dc (US sc).

Round 5: 1 ch, work crab st in first and each st around, join with ss to first st.

Round 6: make number of ch required for cord length. Finish off.

Variations

- Make circular medallion as large or small as desired, increasing as required each round.

- Dry felt a small amount of roving in centre to correspond with photo.

- Pre-thread beads before beginning work and bring them in where desired.

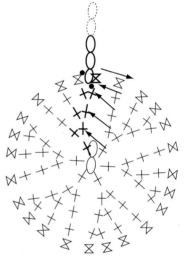

tassel No. 8
circular medallion

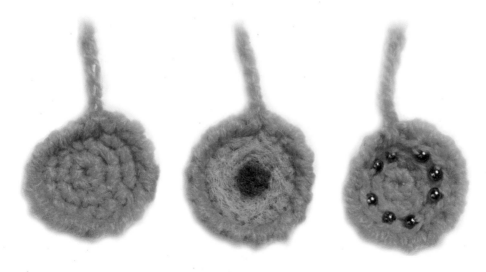

Square medallion tassel

Make 2 ch.

Round 1: 6 dc (US sc) in 2nd ch from hook, do not join, place marker—6 dc (US sc).

Round 2: 2 dc (US sc) in each st around to marker, join with ss to first st—12 dc (US sc).

Round 3: 1 ch, dc (US sc) in same st, *(dc [US sc], 2 ch, dc [US sc]), in next st, dc in each next 2 sts, repeat from * around to last st, dc in last st, join with ss to first st—16 dc (US sc)—4 x 2ch sps.

Round 4: 1 ch, dc (US sc) in same st, dc (US sc) in next st, *3 dc (US sc) in next 2ch sp, dc (US sc) in each next 4 sts, repeat from * to last 2 sts, dc in each last 2 sts, join with ss to first st—28 dc (US sc).

Round 5: 1 ch, work crab st in first and each st around, join with ss to first st.

Round 6: make number of ch required for cord length. Finish off.

Variations

- Make square medallion as large or small as desired.

- Pre-thread beads before beginning work and bring them in where desired.

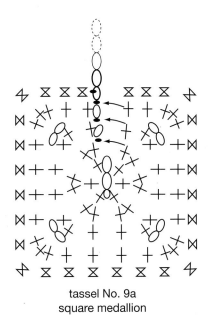

tassel No. 9a
square medallion

Diamond medallion tassel

Work square medallion tassel pattern to end of Round 4.

Round 5: ss back in each st to previous centre st, 1 ch, work crab st in first and each st around, join with ss to first st.

Round 6: make number of ch required for cord length. Finish off.

Variations

□ Make diamond medallion as large or small as desired.

□ Dry felt a small amount of roving in centre to correspond with photo.

□ Pre-thread beads before beginning work and bring them in where desired.

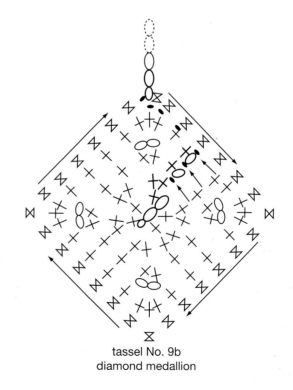

tassel No. 9b
diamond medallion

Triangular medallion tassel

Make 10 ch or any even number required for size desired.

Row 1: dc (US sc) in 2nd ch from hook and in each ch across—9 dc (US sc).

Row 2: 1 ch, turn, dc dec (US sc dec) over first 2 sts, dc (US sc) in each st across to last 2 sts, dc dec (US sc dec) over last 2 sts—3 dc (US sc).

Row 3: repeat Row 2.

Row 4: 1 ch, turn, dc dec (US sc dec) over all 3 sts—1 dc (US sc).

Row 5: 1ch, do not turn, work crab st evenly around, join with ss to first st.

Round 6: make number of ch required for cord length. Finish off.

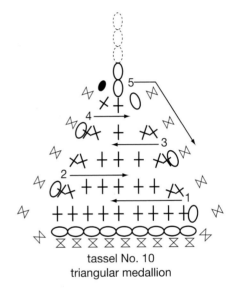

tassel No. 10
triangular medallion

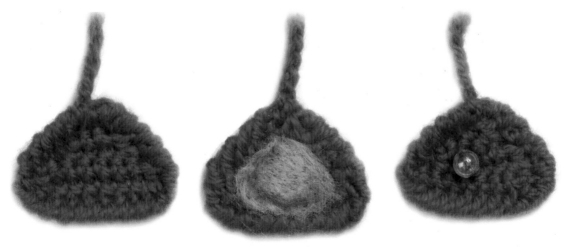

Links tassel A

First link

Make 8 ch or any number required for link size, join with ss to form ring.

Round 1: 1 ch, into ring work 16 dc (US sc) or number required to cover ch ring, join with ss to first st, make number of ch required for cord length. Finish off.

Second and subsequent links

Make 8 ch or any number required for link size, thread chain through first link, join with ss to form ring.

Round 1: 1 ch, into ring work 16 dc (US sc) or number required to cover ch ring, join with ss to first st. Finish off.

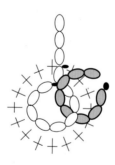

tassel No. 11a
links 1

Links tassel B

First link

Make 8 ch or any number required for link size, join with ss to form ring.

Round 1: 1 ch, into ring work 17 dc (US sc) or other uneven number required to cover ch ring, join with ss to first st. Finish off.

Second and subsequent links

Bring in yarn in 9th dc (US sc) or centre st of previous link, make 8 ch or any number required for link size, remove hook, insert hook from front to back in first ch, bring in dropped ch and join with ss to form ring.

Round 1: 1 ch, into ring work 17 dc (US sc) or other uneven number required to cover ch ring, remove hook, insert hook from back to front in first dc (US sc), bring in dropped ch and join with ss. Finish off.

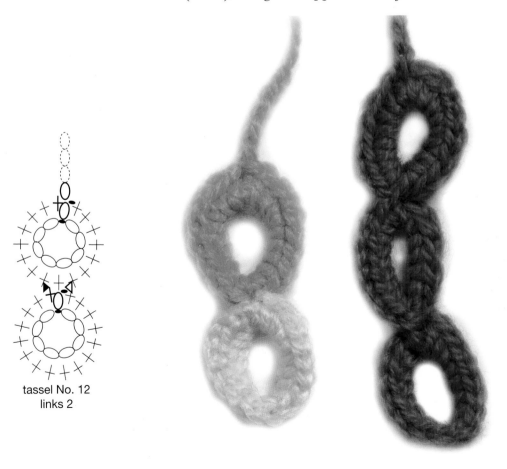

tassel No. 12
links 2

Twisted cord tassel

Bring in yarn where required, make 1 ch (beginning ch), yoh and draw up a long loop about 18 cm (7 in), keep hold of beginning 1 ch with left hand and with right hand twist long loop with hook clockwise until very tight (approx. 20 to 30 times), fold cord in half (it should twist around itself) join with ss to beginning 1 ch.

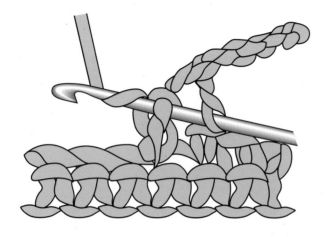

Basic clump tassel

Bring together 6 to 12 lengths of the different yarns used in your project and wind around a piece of card appropriate to length required. Double thread a darning needle with enough yarn to tie off top end and knot or chain into a cord. Pass needle under wound yarn at top of card, pull tight, knot together and make cord. Using sharp scissors, cut through all yarns at bottom of card. Measure approx. 2 cm (1 in) from top and tightly wind another double thread around all cut threads, tie off securely and incorporate tail ends into tassel.

Ponytail clump tassel

Make basic clump tassel as above, then use a very long doubled thread, to extend the binding around the cut threads. Tie off securely and incorporate tail ends into tassel.

This ponytail tassel was wound with a variegated yarn to give the multi-coloured effect.

Felted bead tassel: geometric and freeform shapes
See Chapter 7 for instructions on felting.

As with most things I do when I'm learning something new, I make it over and over again until I get the hang of it. So it was for these felted balls and odd-shaped bits and pieces—I literally had bags of them. Never one to throw anything away, I came upon the idea of using some beading thread, stringing these felted bits together and interlacing each piece with baubles and beads. Another one of those wow 'how-did-you-do-that?' effects.

'What to do with all those ends?'

Where there are groups of tassels so too will there be lots of leftover tail ends—many of which are just too plain and ordinary to leave as they are. You can of course weave them in, never to be seen again, although I find this usually results in a bulky edge that interferes with the drape of the fringe, if not the whole fabric.

You might consider beading or knotting some of these pesky leftovers and turning them into something special. The following suggestions are only a few of the many knots and beading methods available to you— have a look in those old macramé books stashed somewhere in the corner of the shed.

Try adding beads to thinner plies. Leftover tail ends kept deliberately long, then threaded with beads in interesting ways, is a great way of eliminating that tiresome job of weaving them in later and possibly ruining the drape of your garment.

Bundle together groups of threads and tie with a simple overhand knot.

Use a simple overhand knot to secure beads.

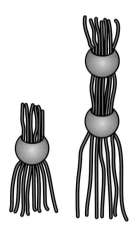

Hint: Shape a firm piece of paper into a cone and wrap around bundled threads for threading large-holed-beads.

Barrel knots look great on their own.

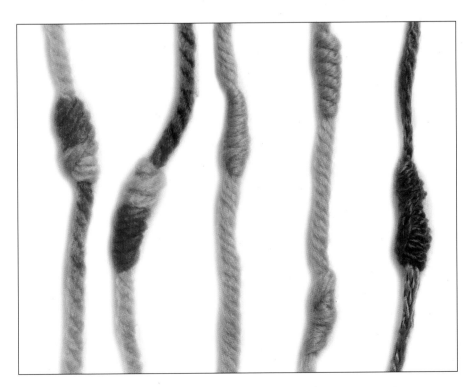

Gallery D
... AND SIMPLY GREAT STUFF

Corsage is a small floral motif with every tail end beaded to the max.

Chocolate Box Using a pre-made cushion cover as a base, numerous freeform patches were sewn directly onto it. Patches of crochet mesh allow the original cover fabric to show through. Over-the-top beading and metallic yarns give this piece an opulent look.

Full Bloom Floral motifs, Vilene-based patches and wet-felted patches and balls were sewn directly onto a pre-made cushion cover to create this piece, again leaving lots of spaces for the original cover fabric to show through. Totally over-the-top, where more is more—you simply can't overdo it.

Tassel on a Rope I and **II:** both began with a 1.8—2 m length of dc (US sc) edged with crab stitch. To these a multitude of tassels were added, with every tail-end threaded with an assortment of glass, metallic and wooden beads.

Regal Mane I made this piece too long originally. I wasn't about to pull it apart, so I decided to make a feature of the overlap at the back. You see, there are no mistakes, only creative adjustments—let's simply call it Art.

Olive Stone This elegant collar or neck piece is worked in Katia Madison yarn and beaded with hand-made, hand-painted polymer and wooden beads.

Purple Pocket was fashioned using an old worn-out vinyl glasses case as the template. Bullion stitch motifs form the front, Tunisian crochet the back and flap. The case was lined with commercial felt.

When I made **T-Cosy** I was having a bit of fun with a largely outmoded yet enduring idea.

Coral Isle From the very beginning as I played around with yarns, stitches, hook sizes, texture, form and colour, I was forever coming up with motifs that reminded me of the ocean, coral reefs in particular. I finally gave in, went with the flow and created this metre square mural. Most of the coral and shell motifs were made individually then sewn or slip-seamed together. The water and sky were crocheted in one piece. When everything was finally joined together, I attached the fabric to a sheet of shade-cloth, and stretched the whole thing over a wooden frame.

7.
A touch of felt and other interesting techniques

This chapter touches on a number of techniques that students often ask me about, most of which I enjoy using in conjunction with freeform. My knowledge of them is by no means extensive and came about, in the main, by simply doing. When a problem arose I'd try something different to see what happened. For embroidery stitches I dug deep into memory, back to my Home Economics days at school. Sometimes the results from a technique I always wanted to try, like felting for example, so delighted me that I just had to find a way of incorporating it into my work. When I complained about my wasteful tail-ends in class one day, a couple of quilters suggested I try making patches with washaway backing fabrics like Vilene. I had a go and another door of possibilities opened. The simple weaving I do is just that—very basic, extremely simple—but I love the texture and the blurring of colours that result and, from time to time, I'll find the very spot for that woven treasure. While going through some old, forgotten and badly neglected macramé books, I came across some interesting knots that I now use all the time. What I'm trying to say—to emphasise—here is that nothing is 'verboten' and anything is possible. Sometimes an idea is sparked by the most unlikely trigger. Just have a go and see what happens—you'll be pleasantly surprised.

Many of these crafts are enjoying revivals (in their own right) so for those of you who require more comprehensive information about any of them, look out for the many excellent publications on each subject available from book stores, libraries and the internet. The information given here I have gathered over the years by reading and attending workshops, asking others how to and, in the case of felting, through hours and hours of play and experimentation at my kitchen sink.

FELTING

I find three felting methods useful in my freeform work—wet felting using carded fleece; wet felting using pre-knitted or crocheted patches; and dry felting, using a felting needle-punch tool to weld pre-made felted and/or crochet/knitted patches together or for adding extra fibre embellishments to any pre-made patch.

I use felted material to add interest—for its distinctive texture and diverse colour hues. I like the way it compliments or contrasts with yarns in a particular project and the way it blends so readily into the freeform technique, often injecting a completely new dimension to my work. I keep felted patches small (about palm size) to retain the freedom of moving them around my template. As a general rule, I'm not too concerned about the shape or even colour placement of a particular patch. I find this lack of control—never being quite sure how it will turn out—exciting. The odd shapes and random colour blends that result often steer or divert the direction of the project in mind.

I find felting creatively absorbing, a diversion from what I normally do, and simply enjoy the break away from the usual crocheting, knitting, sewing and weaving that seems, for the moment, to have taken over my entire creative life.

Of course, this is totally personal and certainly not for everyone, but for those of you who would like to give it a go, following are quick tutorials for making palm-size felt patches that can be incorporated somewhere into your work.

Note: for clarity commercial felt has been used in some of the photo illustrations.

WET FELTING

Wet felt patch made from carded fleece

You will need

Kitchen sink or large basin and an area where you can splash about with access to hot water.

Carded fleece in colours of choice.

Pure soap.

Sponge.

Half a metre (half yard) or so of muslin or thin sheeting cut into two pieces.

A strong waterproof board (plastic chopping board does the trick) to work on.

Rubber gloves if you don't like all that harsh soap and hot water on your hands.

Towels for wringing out excess water.

Technique

1   Divide your carded fleece into three equal portions.

2   Fill the sink with about a litre (1 ½ pints) of the hottest water you can tolerate and work the soap into a lather.

3   Lay one of the pieces of muslin on the board.

4   Assuming you are right-handed, hold the first portion of fleece in your left hand and with fingers and palm of the right pinch off even tufts of fleece, laying them horizontally and in an overlapping fashion across the muslin-covered board to desired size (allow for shrinkage).

5   Repeat pinching technique in the opposite direction with the second portion of fleece.

6   Repeat pinching technique in a vertical direction with last portion of fleece, creating a criss-cross effect with the fibres.

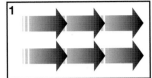  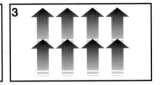

7   Lay the other piece of muslin over the laid-out fleece.

8   Using the sponge, sprinkle the muslin and wool 'sandwich' with hot soapy water and, from the centre out, gently press down with an open palm to eliminate air, being mindful not to disturb the fibres too much and create holes.

9   When muslin is completely flat and wet, again with an open palm, gently rub in a circular motion over the whole piece, continuously sprinkling with hot soapy water.

10   At this stage you can carefully peel away the top muslin layer and add fleece in other colour/s, repeating steps 4, 5 and 6. Replace the muslin and repeat steps 8 and 9.

11   Once all the fibres have meshed (test this by pinching the felt—the fibres should pull up without separating), gently peel away the muslin from both sides and from now on squeeze and rub the felt patch in your hands, continuously dipping it in the hot soapy water. From time to time run it under cold water, then repeat the squeezing and rubbing and continuous dipping in the hot soapy water. The more times you repeat this procedure the thicker the felt patch will become.

12   When you're satisfied that your patch is felted, rinse it well, because soap residue dulls the lustre of the wool and weakens the fibres over time.

13   Roll in a towel and squeeze out excess water. I'm usually happy to let my patches air-dry naturally on a drying rack, although you can pin them into shape if you prefer. Most importantly, they must be completely dry before being incorporated into your work.

Wet felt patch made from carded fleece

Wet felting with pre-made patches

Experimentation with suitable wool is essential. Generally, 100 per cent wool yarn (hand wash only) will felt. I strongly recommend always making tester patches to gauge feltability, colourfastness and shrinkage, and filing them along with the manufacturer's label and a yarn sample in a folder for future reference. Hand felting and machine felting have given me the most consistent results. However, because I usually only make a few patches for a particular project at any one time, my preference is for hand felting. It may take a little more time and muscle power but it's the most water-wise for these small pieces.

Hand felting

You will need

Kitchen sink or large basin and an area where you can splash about with access to hot water.

Pre-made patches.

Pure soap.

Rubber gloves if you don't like all that harsh soap and hot water on your hands.

Towels for wringing out excess water.

Technique

1   Have your pre-made patches ready.

2   Fill sink with about a litre (1 ½ pints) of the hottest water you can tolerate and work soap into a lather.

3   Place the patch into the hot soapy water and rigorously rub and squeeze it in both hands. Keep topping up with hot water and soap. Depending on the wool used, this step requires quite a bit of time and effort before the patch begins to felt. From time to time run it under cold water, then repeat the squeezing and rubbing and continuous dipping in the hot soapy water. The more times you repeat this procedure the thicker the felt patch will become.

4   When you're satisfied your patch is felted, rinse it well, because soap residue dulls the lustre of the wool and weakens the fibres over time.

5   Roll in a towel and squeeze out excess water. I'm usually happy to let my patches air-dry naturally on a drying rack, although you can pin them into shape if you prefer. Most importantly, they must be completely dry before being incorporated into your work.

Machine felting

You will need

Top-loading washing machine.

Pure liquid soap detergent or pure soap flakes.

Pair of jeans or overalls for added agitation.

Towels for wringing out excess water.

Technique

1   Have your pre-knitted/crochet patches ready.

2   Set machine at lowest water level and hottest cycle.

3   Place all your patches in machine together with soap and the jeans or overalls and run machine for about 15—20 minutes or until patches have felted—the time can vary depending on the wool used, so check on how thing are progressing every 5 minutes or so.

4   When you're satisfied with your patches, rinse them well, because soap residue dulls the lustre of the wool and weakens the fibres over time.

5   Roll in a towel and squeeze out excess water. I'm usually happy to let my patches air-dry naturally on a drying rack, but you can pin them into shape if you prefer. Most importantly, they must be completely dry before being incorporated into your work.

Before and after: wet felting with a pre-made patch

DRY FELTING (NEEDLE FELTING)

It must be noted that this not a technique for unsupervised children or anyone with an unsteady hand. The needles have tiny barbs that are exceedingly sharp and will inflict substantial damage where fingers get in the way, especially when used singly without the punch applicator.

Although I prefer pure wool and carded fleece for this method, through experimentation I have successfully dry-felted all types of wool/acrylic blends. However, do try to avoid yarns with high percentages of polyester, viscose, nylon, Lurex and metallic fibres, as the needles tend to cut and break the fibres rather than felt. But here again, I still emphasise the need to experiment—interesting and amazing effects can arise from the most unlikely yarns.

Use the dry felting method to weld felted patches to pre-made patches. This effectively produces an almost invisible seam; it is difficult to discern where the felting ends and the crochet or knitted background begins. Dry-felt tufts of carded fleece directly onto a patch whose colour or texture is dull or uninteresting. Individual crochet motifs (round bullions, for example) can be dry-felted to an existing felted, crochet or knitted patch.

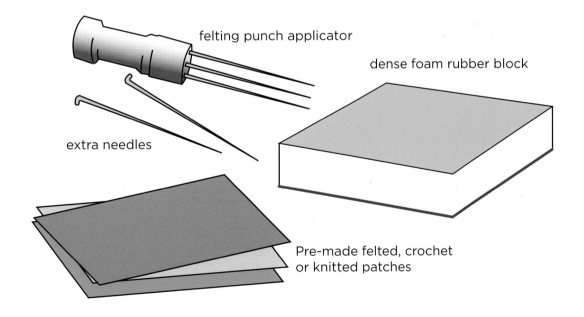

felting punch applicator

dense foam rubber block

extra needles

Pre-made felted, crochet or knitted patches

Equipment used in dry felting

You will need

Complete dry felting punch applicator with needles and some single needles.

Pre-made felted, crochet or knitted patches or carded fleece, depending on what you plan to do.

Felting needle mat or dense foam rubber block at least 15 cm (6 in) square x 5 cm (2 in) thick.

Technique

Follow the directions supplied by the manufacturer of the dry felting punch applicator.

A few tips I've picked up along the way

- Always test a yarn before incorporating it into your project.

- Work the felting needles, whether as the punch applicator or singly, in a straight up-and-down motion. The needles are brittle and can easily snap if twisted or bent.

- Keep working until fibres are visible on the underside of the patch.

- Use the felting punch applicator to get started then finish off with a single needle to ensure a solid weld.

- Use the felting punch applicator for large areas.

- For individual motifs, work single needle around edge of motif to ensure even and solid attachment.

- Never work on wet or damp patches—wet fibres are tough and can cause needles to snap.

- A light spray of spray starch and a warm iron will give a smooth, flat finish to needle-felted carded felt.

- Regularly clean the felting punch applicator to prevent lint build-up.

- Regularly clean the needle felting mat or foam rubber block to prevent lint and fibre build-up.

- Concentrate, keep your wits about you when using the single needle—it really hurts when you jab your finger.

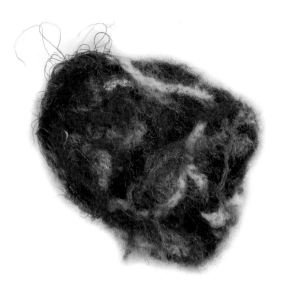 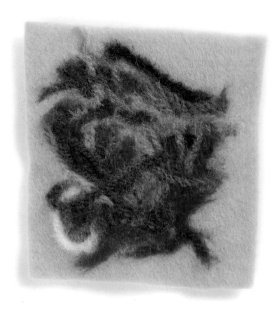

Left: Dry felted tail ends

Right: Tail ends dry felted onto commercial felt

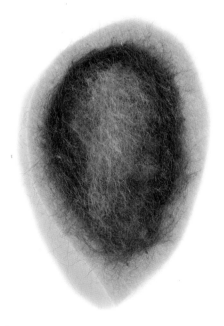 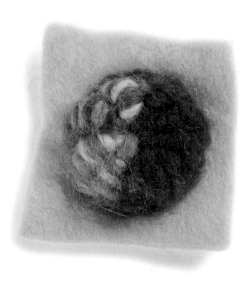

Left: Carded fleece dry felted onto commercial felt

Right: Round bullion dry felted onto commercial felt

WASHAWAY FABRIC PATCHES

Vilene may be the best known of these; similar products include Dissolve, Solvy, Aqua Film and Rinseaway. I use Vilene, a water-soluble stabiliser and embroidery and lace-making aide that can be hand or machine sewn then rinsed away with water, as just another way of bring interesting texture and colour to my work. I've always loathed throwing anything away, with the result that over the years I've collected little bags full of tail-ends in the hope of one day finding a use for them. Presto! The washaway fabric technique was just the ticket.

Technique

1   Gather together tail ends and place on Vilene in an arrangement that pleases the eye, then using a bright, shiny thread (quilter's cottons are great for this) machine sew every-which-way across the patch.

2   When you've arrived at the desired effect, rinse the patch in water until all Vilene has dissolved.

3   Roll in a towel and squeeze out excess water. I'm usually happy to let my patches air-dry naturally on a drying rack, although you can pin them into shape if you prefer. Most importantly, they must be completely dry before being incorporated into your work.

Lay tail ends on Vilene & machine sew every-which-way over patch

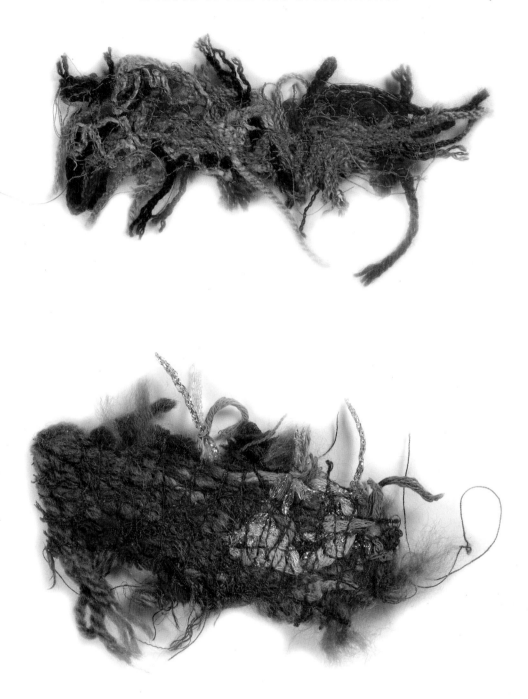

Tail end patches after Vilene has been washed away then air dried
and ready to be incorporated into your freeform work

EMBROIDERY

While on the subject of different techniques, it's worth bringing your attention to the wonderful array of embroidery stitches that can be incorporated into your freeform work. Experiment to your heart's content here—you'll be delighted with the results of combining traditional stitches with unconventional yarns. The following are some of my favourite and most often used embroidery stitches—but don't be limited by my choice here, there so many more to choose from. No doubt avid embroiders and lace-makers will have a multitude of other ideas, uses for Vilene and a more comprehensive stitch library, so go for it—you'll be amazed by what you can do.

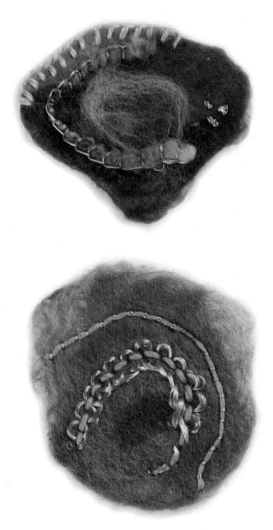

Wet felted patches embroidered with blanket stitch, Chinese lace stitch & some couching stitches to add detail and interest or liven up a dull space

Incorporate any of the following stitches to jazz up a dull, uninteresting spot—try some metallics, glittery or vivid silk yarns. These are but a sample of the many stitches available. Keep in mind, in line with the freeform technique, working stitches in a haphazard fashion, staying away as much as possible from straight lines. Follow seams, work across an area and continue into another. Work with two yarns at the same time—mix metallic and cotton, bright with dull, harmonise or contrast, smooth over rough in the case of couching—the combinations are exciting and endless.

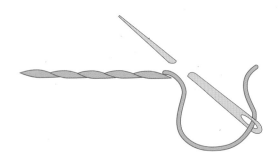

Stem stitch: great for outlining. Use extra bright or metallic thread.

Simple chain stitch: work across a dull uninteresting area.

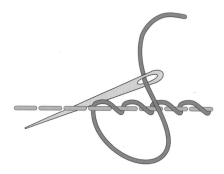

Overcast running stitch: ideal for highlighting unused loops with extra bright or metallic thread.

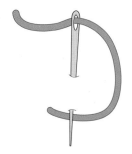 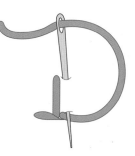 

Buttonhole stitch: use around edges or tidy unsightly joins.

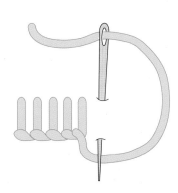

Blanket stitch: use around edges of felted patches as a base from which you can crochet or knit.

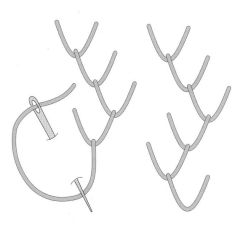

Feather stitch: looks great using variegated yarn.

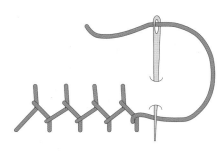

Cretan stitch: another stitch that looks great using variegated yarn.

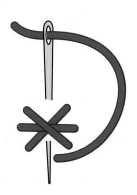

Long stitch star.

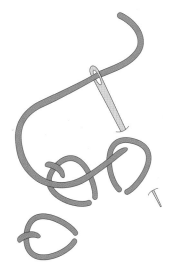

Lazy daisy stitch.

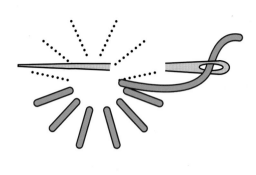

Long stitch daisy.

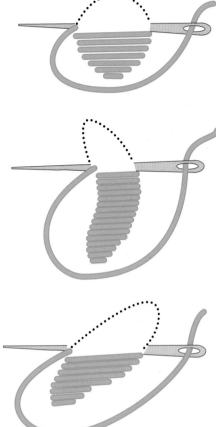

Satin stitch.

Herringbone stitch: looks terrific using
metallic yarn.

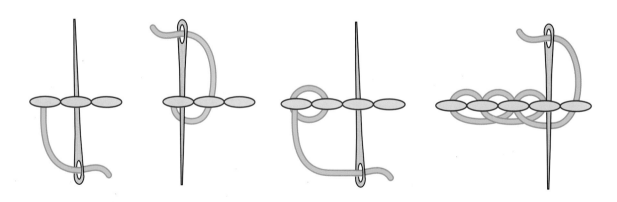

Chinese lace: looks fabulous using metallic yarns to glitz up a dull area, but also see what
happens when you use 12-ply or two yarns together across a plain crochet/knit area.

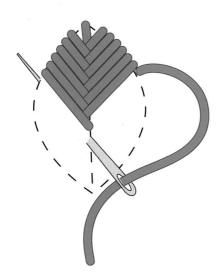

Fishbone stitch.

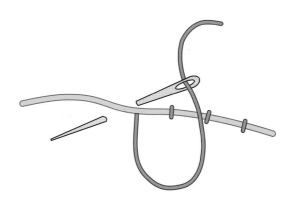

Simple couching stitch.
One yarn lies free on the surface and another yarn is used to tack it down. Use contrasting yarns, ribbons, cords. I love this stitch for its versatility; it's one of my favourites.

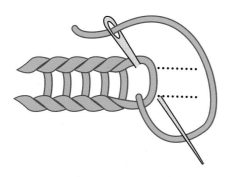

Roman chain stitch: love it for metallic yarn also.

Herringbone couching stitch.

Roman chain couching stitch.

Blanket couching stitch.

BASIC WEAVING

Weaving is a complex and highly skilled craft. Accomplished spinners and weavers may, quite rightly, cringe at the primitive tools I use to make my little patches. But, because all the pieces I'll ever need for my projects are so small (I'll never be weaving a mountain of fabric) these simple tools and methods give me consistently excellent results. Woven patches bring another texture to your project.

Effective woven patches can be created using a simple card loom, pin or nail loom, embroidery hoop or even an old picture frame. They can be incorporated into your work in the same way as any other patch—when made as a starter patch, pick up a few stitches along an edge and crochet or knit for a bit, creating a space where a bullion motif can be attached, and so on.

As you can see there's not a lot of outlay—so, if you're tempted, there's nothing preventing you from having a go.

Terminology: *warp* refers to a continuous yarn threaded lengthwise; *weft* refers to a yarn woven horizontally across the warp.

You will need

Yarn: be adventurous here; try felted wool or silk tops, fuzzy, lumpy, smooth yarn, weave two or more at the same time, mix in some metallic or glittery yarns and so on. Just mix them up and see what happens.

Loom: refers to a strong frame or board with tacks or pins placed at equal intervals to hold the warp. There are several types: stretcher bar frame—an old picture frame will do here; cardboard loom—the advantage of this is that it can be cut into odd shapes; pin or nail loom, which is also ideal for odd shapes; an embroidery hoop is a ready resource, but requires a bit of fiddling with the warp.

Shuttle: to carry the weft through the warp threads; you can use a long, large-eyed blunt needle, or a handmade cardboard needle.

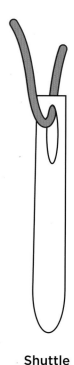

Shuttle

Beater: this is used to push the weft into place; you can use a wide-toothed comb, fork, strong cardboard strips, wooden ruler.

Other essential bits and pieces include: tacks and strong pins, scissors, tape measure, blunt needles.

Technique

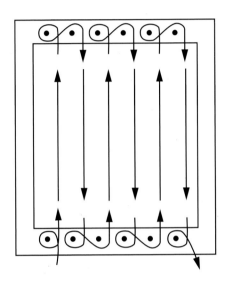 

Left: Winding on the warp on a stretcher bar frame loom.

Right: Weaving in the weft on a stretcher bar frame loom.

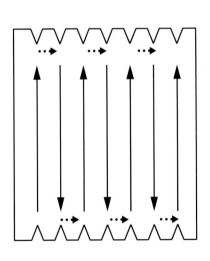 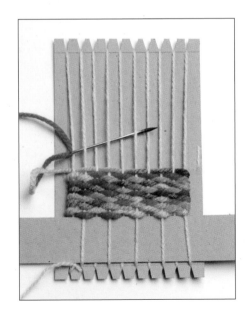

Left: Winding on the warp on a cardboard loom.

Right: Weaving in the weft on a cardboard loom.

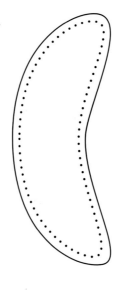

Left: Embroidery hoop as loom. Right: Cardboard pin loom.

Woven patches incorporating couching stitch and blanket stitch embroidery, varying sized bullions around an edge, some surface crochet embellishments and a couple of round bullions in appropriate spaces.